Contents

PART III Reflections on Process / 111

Contributors

Brian Adams is Language Arts Coordinator and teacher at Simon Fraser Junior High School, Calgary, Alberta.

Michelle Bastock is at St. Thomas Aquinas School in Calgary, Alberta, teaching grade one.

Wendy Chamberlain teaches at Edgemont School, Calgary, Alberta.

Victoria Conrad teaches in the Transition School for junior high school dropouts operated by the Calgary Board of Education in Calgary, Alberta.

Angie Craigie teaches fourth grade at Edgemont School in Calgary, Alberta.

Naomi Dahl is currently on professional improvement leave from her role as Assistant Principal with the Calgary Board of Education.

Margaret H. Hajdu teaches English at Senator Riley High School in High River, Alberta.

Marian R. Hood is a high school English teacher at Dr. E. P. Scarlett High School in Calgary, Alberta.

Debbie Huitema teaches at Jerry Potts Elementary School in Calgary, Alberta.

Blanche Lamont is Assistant Principal and grade five teacher at Killarney Elementary School in Calgary, Alberta.

Cheryl A. Lemire is a corrective learning teacher for grades one through six at Brébeuf School in Calgary, Alberta.

Terry MacKenzie is Assistant Principal and grade five teacher at Earl Grey Elementary School in Calgary, Alberta.

Beverly MacLean is a grade five teacher at Percy Pegler Elementary School in Okotoks, Alberta.

Toni L. Marasco is the Principal of Mother Teresa School in Calgary, Alberta.

Debra Morgan is a teacher at Marion Carson Elementary School, Calgary, Alberta.

Peggy Murakami has a grade one class at Terrace Road Elementary School, Calgary, Alberta.

Judy Osinski teaches at Sir James Lougheed Elementary School, Calgary, Alberta.

Diane Perry teaches at Marion Carson Elementary School, Calgary, Alberta.

Myrna Reeves is Consultant, School Library Programs, Department of Curriculum, Calgary Board of Education, Calgary, Alberta.

Linda F. Steen is a teacher-librarian at Marion Carson Elementary School, Calgary, Alberta.

Barbara C. Wallace is Supervisor of Curriculum with Foothills School Division in High River, Alberta.

Carla Watson has a grade two class at Percy Pegler Elementary School in Okotoks, Alberta.

Kathleen Weir is a high school English teacher at Sir Winston Churchill High School, Calgary, Alberta.

Sandra Wenz teaches at Edgemont School, Calgary, Alberta.

Susan West is a language arts teacher at A. E. Cross Junior High School, Calgary, Alberta.

Introduction

Joining Others on New Journeys to Communities of Readers

"What is it that I do when I read?" asks a teacher while reflecting on how to evoke a classroom setting where reading can be naturally personal and social.

I think about how I read — immersing myself into my book — *my* book, the one *I* have chosen myself, passing my solitary time living the mysteries of the characters' lives. I think about how I decide to race through clumps of pages or, at times, decide simply to pause to contemplate and dream. I think of how I pass my books on and of how I suggest them to others.

Then I remember how books come to me — often from friends and colleagues who recommend them. So I read widely: South African André Brink's *States of Emergency* for its challenge and its social significance, *The Greek Key* by Colin Forbes for adventure and release, and the Canadian Fionavar trilogy for amazement and fantasy. Some books come by chance, but only because I am open to their arrival, open because I see myself as a part of a community of readers, a community that extends back through all my years and to all the places I have lived, a community with endless possibilities that gives me access to the magic of faraway places, other times, and the lives of others.

I am not alone in thinking, with some surprise, wonder and pleasure, about how this enjoyment of reading has come about. I am not alone in considering how it might come about for others, for the students of teachers I know, or for my own students.

Nancie Atwell puts into words that which many of us have been ruminating over:

> For a long time, the same groups of students who sat at their own big desks each day in writing workshop returned to my room each day when it came time for reading to find me barricaded behind my big desk. Writing was something students did, and literature was something I did to students.... I made all the choices, took all the responsibility and found all the meanings.... Finally, I did something I should have known to do long before. I matched my own reading process against the reading process I enforced in my classroom. It was not a very close fit. For example, I usually decide what I'll read, but my students seldom decided for themselves.... They read at the pace I set, often fragmented bits and pieces of text at a time, looking for the answers I wanted to the questions I posed.... What I did as an adult reader had little to do with what I asked of my kids....
> —*Nancie Atwell (1987, pp. 19, 20)*

As more and more of us began to think about what *we* do when *we* read, we began the journey that led to this book, a journey of thinking about the nature of what it is to read and to be a reader, a journey of thinking about what it is to teach and to learn, to model and to lead.

For most of the teacher-writers in this book the impetus to begin this journey began with reflection upon what was happening in their classrooms. Nancie Atwell's words quoted above seem to summarize a good portion of that reflection. Some of us "met" Nancie Atwell when Blanche Lamont (see pages 24–43) brought her to our attention. As Blanche consulted with her fellow Calgary teachers she introduced the concept of Readers' Workshops. From then on, in the amazing and wondrous ways that teachers have, the ideas spread and were elaborated. Perhaps we might imagine Charlotte spinning one of her webs; certainly the pattern of infectious enthusiasm is now impossible to retrace.

If there is *one* constant that has led those of us whose articles appear in this book to change our practices, then it is that *as teachers we embrace uncertainties*. We embrace the uncertainty that is involved in "forever wondering...." By doing so we open up our own possibilities for change, and even for transformation of who we are as teachers when we are in our reading-writing classrooms. We open up the possibilities of transforming what we would be doing with the others in our classrooms — how we would work with our students in particular.

To find the personal and professional security to let go of other methods, of other "certainties" of classroom practice, we turned to professional reading *and* to one another. As you read the accounts in this book the traces of influence from one person to another will be apparent at times. Sometimes, however, it is not immediately obvious that a teacher read and reread Nancie Atwell's book, or that a teacher checked and re-checked with his or her language arts consultant, or that he or she telephoned a colleague in another school regularly for reassurance.

In the spring of 1989, teachers with the Calgary Board of Education sponsored a Saturday session on Readers' Workshops to which eighty teachers came. From then on a kind of "movement" seemed to grow. As teachers requested information about Readers' Workshops it became evident that our random collections of articles would no longer suffice. Moreover, not *every* teacher wanted to make the *same* journey of discovery. As it became known that more and more teachers could describe how they were implementing their particular Readers' Workshops and *why* they dared to try to do so, the Calgary and District Council, International Reading Association, helped to prepare a collection of pieces about Readers' Workshops. It was out of that collection that this book grew.

Like many of you, when we set out on our journey most of us were teachers who were in the midst of teaching. We felt that we already knew much about reading and books, our particular students and their needs, curricular demands, and classroom life. Nevertheless, as we pondered more closely the processes of reading, we were all led to try new approaches to the "teaching" of reading in our classrooms. What we are trying to do in the pieces in this book is to share, in our various ways, the how and why of our transformed practices.

Most of us built upon what we were already doing to teach reading by talking with others and by professional reading, as well as by discovering, after just "giving it a go," that Readers' Workshops do indeed work. While we were all unique in what we knew and needed, and while we went about becoming advocates of Readers' Workshops in different ways, when we united our professional readings, our in-service learnings, our colleagues' ideas, and our own practices, we found that we all had a feeling of having "come home."

We found that we wanted to share our stories, to share our excitement and our ideas. But at the same time, we wanted to avoid developing an orthodoxy about Readers' Workshops by demonstrating that there are many ways to put our understandings and beliefs into practice. We wanted to give access to a variety of teachers' ways of thinking that allowed for various types of workshops to emerge in different settings. Because we know that each person must adapt to local conditions, we wanted to point to the core principles of Readers' Workshops that guide us. Rather than providing clear recipes for classroom practice (which rarely worked for us), we seek to share how we have applied these core principles. We hope that "Readers' Workshops," as an expression, serves to suggest that there are many versions of workshops, and that you will read what follows with the intention of revitalizing your own practice, not of seeking a new orthodoxy.

Regardless of the approach taken to Readers' Workshops by each of the teacher-writers represented in this book, the book provides models of classroom environments that are clearly designed to empower learners to read successfully, and to stimulate them to feel in control of their comprehension. The writers also hope to support others in their move towards using new methods to lead students to literacy.

The book presents pieces by teacher-writers whose students range from the advantaged and well prepared to the needy and deprived. We have found that the core principles of Readers' Workshops apply to all students regardless of background and ability and so we have not tried to separate the experiences with one group of students from the experiences with another.

Some of the pieces reveal the writers' awareness of going through stages of development and growth with Readers' Workshops. For most, the workshop format meant making a dramatic change in who had control over choice, time and responsibility. For all, it meant a confrontation with how meaning gets "made" in reading, and with how readers respond to books, poems, and stories. And for all of us, Readers' Workshops meant that we learned from our students as much as our students learned from us.

Implicitly, the writers are all tackling the question of the role of a teacher. We think that there is room within the image of a *workshop* for teachers to act as facilitators or guides, drawing upon their knowledge of literature and language learning, and simultaneously for teachers to explain and to demonstrate to their students. From presenting mini-lessons or book talks, from developing students' understanding with conferences and journals, emerge the range of roles that are natural for teachers.

Every article in this book comes from a unique teaching-learning situation, so that it can be seen as that teacher's story of how he or she is becoming a different teacher, seeing and valuing students in some different manner. Some of the pieces may inspire some of you to start out on your own journeys to communities of readers; others will encourage and reinforce the enthusiasm of those of you who are already working with Readers' Workshops; and some pieces may cause you to argue or question.

Because of the specific nature of some of the pieces, you may find that dipping into our book, selecting the portions that particularly apply to you, will be the best way to let it influence your own thinking.

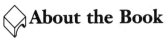

About the Book

In Part I of *Readers' Workshops*, "Building from an Informed Base," you will learn about the open "model" we have for Readers' Workshops, what the core principles are, and why we believe they are worth considering. We also hope that you will see how, for us, our personal reflections on reading and our disposition to observe our students carefully helped us to decide to try these workshops with our students. A key article by Blanche Lamont describes the elements of a Readers' Workshop while also giving practical suggestions for possible teachers' mini-lessons within the workshop context.

In Part II, "Workshops for Success," are accounts of teachers from first grade through secondary school taking on and using various workshop approaches in their classrooms. There are several pieces that will help you to get started. The writers suggest varying degrees of teacher involvement in the getting-started process, depending in large part on the students involved, for example, special populations such as primary students and special needs' readers. Part II is the most "practical" section of our book.

Part III, "Reflections on Process," will help you to step back and evaluate the effectiveness of Readers' Workshops and of the student response tools that are integral to them. Accounts from elementary and secondary teachers enrich this section also.

Finally, Part IV, "Resources to Bridge Literature and Literacy," is offered as one way to continue with the learning we find is required of us when we embrace literature-based programs. Within the resources are professional materials that influenced the ways of thinking of our writers.

If you have chosen to read this collection of articles, then you have joined our community of learners, learning about yourself as a teacher and about Readers' Workshops as possible images for creating strong, motivated readers.

T. M.

References

Atwell, Nancie. 1987. *In the Middle: Writing, Reading, and Learning with Adolescents*. Portsmouth, NH: Boynton/Cook Publishers Inc.

PART

I

Building from an Informed Base

Without Stones There Is No Arch: Building Bridges to Communities of Readers

Terry MacKenzie's career includes teaching, clinical and consultative work in five provinces from kindergarten through university levels, as well as three years recently as an elementary language arts consultant for the Calgary Board of Education. Now, after a year of graduate school, he is meeting new challenges teaching fifth-graders, as well as being an assistant principal.

Bridges intrigue me. Graceful steel ones fly over vastness, barely seeming to be supported. Log bridges plod across ravines, heavy with their own woodwork. Others mysteriously spring out of the road ahead and lift us across turbulent rivers. Always, they represent getting across an obstacle, smoothing the way and helping the traveller.

While reading not long ago, I came across these lines:

Marco Polo describes a bridge, stone by stone.

"But which is the stone that supports the bridge?" Kublai Khan asks.

"The bridge is not supported by one stone or another," Marco answers, "but by the line of the arch that they form."

Kublai remains silent, reflecting. Then he adds: "Why do you speak to me of the stones? It is only the arch that matters to me."

Polo answers: "Without stones there is no arch."

—*Italo Calvino (1972, p. 82)*

Marco Polo chose to describe the individual stones, yet for Kublai Khan only the arch is of interest. A tension pulls within their dialogue. Simultaneously, they need to speak both of the whole bridge and of the supportive stones. Khan and Polo are discovering through their conversation that the arch and the stones matter *together*.

As a metaphor for Readers' Workshops, the image of a bridge arching across a space represents a way to bring students through the journey to the exciting world of being a reader. In seeking to talk about and to understand Readers' Workshops, we come across the same tension between the parts and the whole. The stones are the principles that are the foundation of Readers' Workshops; the arch is the direction or purpose of the Workshops — towards literacy.

Life in Readers' Workshops

Eyes flash! Voices chatter! The air seems to quiver. An excitement permeates the gatherings of teachers who are changing their classrooms, their roles and their beliefs in order to build authentic bridges to literacy for their students to cross. Whether as a result of discussions with colleagues, or their own classroom experiences and reflections, or professional reading, these teachers are working to create places for learning where students are involved and engaged. As these teachers watch their students choosing their own books, reading books, talking about books, sharing books, and loving books, they describe their amazement at it all. Something is in the air it seems, some way of thinking that is grounded in evolving and compelling beliefs and assumptions about reading and learning and teaching.

What is going on? These teachers are sharing the excitement of seeing Readers' Workshops in action.

Why has a *workshop* image been chosen for Readers' Workshops? A workshop depicts many people busily going about their purposeful tasks — making or creating something for someone. Every person is doing something of value, sometimes alone, sometimes in cooperation with a workmate, sometimes working in one area, sometimes moving about.

There is predictability and routine, in order that invention and creation can flourish. People help one another to do their jobs better — by sharing information and ideas, by working together to overcome problems and by inventing new ways of doing things. Results are exhibited, shared and celebrated.

How do we imagine life in Readers' Workshops?

Readers' Workshops are opportunities for allowing our students to become readers and to continue to grow as readers: choosing their own books, spending time reading and talking about them, responding to them from their own hearts and experiences, and recommending them to one another.

There is no one "correct" way to implement Readers' Workshops. They may be part of the classroom all year or they may be run as though they were "theme units" for shorter periods of time. Moreover, teachers may well change and continue to change the format of their particular workshops as they gain experience, react to their students' changing needs, and evaluate what is or is not working. No matter how the workshops are structured, in all cases the belief in both personal reading and personal response to make meaning — to compose and to comprehend through reading — pervades that classroom all year.

In Readers' Workshops students will be immersed in a wide variety of written texts as their "tools" to make meaning. They will sometimes do this meaning-making just for themselves. As often, they will share meanings with others. Learners may work alone, or they may gain insight from talking, reading and writing with others. They know that there is regular, daily or predictable time to go about this reading, writing and talking. When they are together with their reading materials or their own stories, they demonstrate to one another how they handle difficulties they have had with their reading or with their writing about their reading. They celebrate their meaning-making when the class gathers to hear about one another's books. They celebrate by sharing the results of book projects with dramatizations and displays. A bonding of readers happens as the students use their "cultural tool kits" (Bruner 1986) of language, of art and drama, of human interaction to construct personal interpretations of text.

When you look in on a Readers' Workshop — no matter what form it takes — you will see many different things going on. But you are sure to see students reading in groups, students reading alone, students choosing books alone and with their groups, students writing personal responses to their reading experiences in response journals or writing dialogue letters back and forth to one another about their stories, poems and books, as well as students presenting and recommending what they have read to their community of readers.

Within a Readers' Workshop, students receive instruction in the form of mini-lessons from the teacher or from other students. The teacher is active, but is so in a collaborative, not a directive, manner — guiding students to literature, helping students to read, conferring with them individually or in small groups, teaching the whole class, reading and writing in students' response journals, and demonstrating by their own reading and writing during the workshop what a "real" reader does.

Looking in on a Readers' Workshop, at first you might not see the behind-the-scenes work done by the teacher to bring out the importance of talking about books and to "teach" students how to discuss them, to reveal different ways of responding to literature, to ensure that there are multiple copies of engaging books or stories available to the students, and to develop a responsible, interactive atmosphere in the room. Similarly you would need to observe the workshop over time to discover how the teacher weaves information about literary devices into the students' ongoing acts of meaning-making, and then helps students recognize and value different forms of literature.

This workshop image comes into being with teacher thought and preparation.

The kind of thinking being displayed by teachers who have begun to use Readers' Workshops represents a dramatic change from the days when we acted as supports for prescribed reading programs. Readers' Workshops are response-oriented, literature-based reading approaches to "teaching" reading. In Readers' Workshops, our roles as teachers involve facilitating and supporting rather than dispensing knowledge, correcting "wrong" answers, or interpreting "correctly" the printed words. Rather than supporting particular reading programs, we want the books in our classrooms to support what *we* are doing. And what we are trying to do is to provide an atmosphere in which students can become readers who *choose* to read, readers whose lives are affected by their reading and who enjoy reading. Our hope is to help our students become readers who know that they have control over their ways of making meaning. Our readers should leave us with a sense of being able to react to what they read, to appreciate, to question, to critique, to wonder and to challenge.

When we are creating our own workshops, it is helpful to hold in mind an image of Readers' Workshop similar to the description above and, if possible, to visit a Readers' Workshop in action. But is keeping the image of a workshop in mind or watching a workshop in action enough to let us start our own workshops? Some time ago, a fellow teacher lamented what might go wrong if teachers tried "to do" Readers' Workshops without having read the theoretical background. I personally am not convinced that there is a single theory, a particular writer we should read, or one image that we must have before starting out.

Discovering on our own how to begin Readers' Workshops with our students means that our own self-inquiry, our own ongoing assessment of our beliefs and practices and our own thoughtful problem solving will drive the change in how we teach to a deeper level. By "having a go" at it, we are led to wonder why, and then to seek justification in solid convictions about the conditions for reading growth. But whether the theory builds the practice or the practice constructs the theory, the result eventually should be a kind of togetherness of both. "Without stones there is no arch."

◇ The Foundation Stones for Readers' Workshops: Bridges to Reading

Reading is a relationship between a human being and a text, and the purpose of the activity involves the whole person. To ask what kinds

of readers we hope our young people will become is to ask what kinds of human beings we hope they will become.
— Louise M. Rosenblatt (1983, p. 118)

Several principles serve as the foundation stones for the practices that can be grouped as Readers' Workshops. These principles rest on strongly held views of what it is to be a reader and what it takes to "teach" someone to become a reader — views that have grown out of a history of thought, research, and practice.

For us, the principles that guide the development of our Readers' Workshops are *authenticity, immersion, shared responsibility, meaning-making, risks and approximations, demonstration, community,* and *celebration.* It is these foundation stones that let us take on the special kind of thinking that allows for Readers' Workshops.

Others may call these principles by different names or may suggest additional principles. That would encourage us. The principles underlying Readers' Workshops ought to be ongoing and generative — able to reflect the excitement and evolving nature of the workshop as research in the field and our own practice in the classroom continue to teach us more and more about how the teaching of reading works in different contexts.

A first stone — to read well: *authenticity*

But the teaching should be organized in such a way that reading and writing are necessary for something.
— L. S. Vygotsky (1978, p. 117)

Reading is a meaning-making enterprise in Readers' Workshops. That is, students read for the prime purpose of making meanings with the texts presented to them. To make meaning effectively, they have to be reading "real" writing. By "real" writing we mean writing that speaks specifically to children's and young adults' emotions, their life experiences, their imaginations, and their minds. A lack of such authenticity is found in many of the existing controlled vocabulary basal readers used at the elementary level. As Charlotte Huck writes, "The [trade] books are here and we need to learn to use them not as supplementary to basal readers, but as the very heart of the reading program" (1987, p. 375). And, at the secondary level, comes the realization that focusing on the long-taught selection of literary works may be denying today's young people accessibility to other literature that has personal power for them.

Authentic literature for children and young adults motivates them to engage in reading. Our students know what is meaningful for them and as they are given opportunities to read "real" literature they come to know for themselves the excitement of the "I can't put it down" feeling.

But the principle of authenticity is not an easy principle to implement. It will require us as teachers to read many more books so that we can make appropriate suggestions to the students. It will require us to listen carefully to all the signs from our students that what we are offering them to read is indeed — to them — worth reading. And it requires us to be aware of the different needs of readers at different times in their development.

Carefully chosen stones: *immersed in literature*

> Literature, not reading lessons, teaches children to read in ways that no basal reader can, because literature is read...with passion, with desire.
>
> *—Margaret Meek (1982, p. 290)*

When we pursue ways to bring authenticity to our Readers' Workshops, we learn through personal experience that literature of certain types is needed to *engage* our readers. To provide our students with the opportunities for getting hooked into reading means that we must fulfill the principle of *immersion* in "text-rich" settings. This sort of setting contains more than just a prescribed text. It contains a wide range of literature of all sizes, shapes and genres that is appropriate for the reader, that involves and is real enough emotionally and narratively to result in re-reading and reflecting. And there needs to be lots of it and there needs to be easy access to it.

Meeting the demands of the principle of immersion can be challenging. Access supposes *time* — not only to read, but to reread and to reflect, to be immersed in the reading, not just to be surrounded by books. When we decide to develop a workshop we are forced to make decisions about what to give up and what to change so that we can give the students the necessary time to be immersed in their reading and thinking.

But time is only one resource. Attention to the need for immersion in a text-rich setting also ends up affecting our decisions about planning, and about purchasing resources. It pushes us into confrontations with our knowledge of and awareness of literature and response. As more and more of us become immersed in the phenomena of workshop approaches, many of us are setting up study groups, reading voraciously, and often spending our own money on children's books and young adult literature. We are collaborating with our school librarians, teaching colleagues, and parents to find ways to buy books and to extend the library collections. We are discovering that even the sometimes restricted reading lists in our schools can be expanded when we help policy-makers and curriculum designers to understand the potential of a text-rich setting.

Building together: *shared responsibility*

> ...a constructivist view...implies an active learner who does not passively inhale and retain knowledge as encountered but instead attends to and interprets experience actively, selectively. It is in this sense that knowledge is constructed — individuals perceive, organize, and retain their experience in a unique fashion.
> — *Marianne Amarel (quoted in Janet Emig 1990, p. 92)*

Sharing responsibility for reading is another fundamental principle of Readers' Workshops. A sharing of responsibility shows up in a number of ways in the workshop setting.

We, as teachers, draw on our understandings of reading process, of literature, of learning, and of our particular students in order to create the opportunities for the students to encounter worthwhile texts, to make the texts their own, and to respond to them.

Our students too share responsibility for reading. Over time they discover that they are responsible for making their own meanings from their reading. "Just tell us what it means," demands a high school student of his teacher, who reflects on her beliefs once again as a result of the student's demand. "I just won't tell them what it means to me; they'll think that what I say is *the* meaning." This teacher has confronted the traditional authoritarian view of teaching literature with her own democratic view of a response-based classroom. Her approach reflects the findings of Louise Rosenblatt: "Meaning does not reside ready-made in the text or in the reader; it happens during the transaction between reader and text" (1989, p. 157). So, with the principle of shared responsibility, we find that the reader and the text also share the responsibility for the making of meaning. Furthermore, the responsibility extends to the readers using the meanings they have constructed for further reflection and analysis (Rosenblatt 1990, p. 106). Readers are expected to play with their own interpretations, to really make the meaning their own.

While our reluctance to dictate our own interpretations of literature may be seen as an abandonment of our students to their own devices, or of the text to just any interpretation, the principle of shared responsibility reminds us that our role is, through conversation and questioning, wondering and suggesting, to bring our students to a sense that they can make their own meaning as they read the text and as they contemplate what they read. We help them balance the text and their thinking with our own understandings. But we ensure that they work with the text, not just with our interpretations of it — nor indeed with just their own individual interpretations of it.

Hand-crafted stones: *readers making meaning*

> Whatever comes out, let nothing we do stand between reader and author, for we are parasitic middlemen, when all is said and done.
> —*Margaret Meek (1982, p. 291)*

"What does this poem mean?" asks the textbook, the teacher, the exam — a seemingly open question until we examine the questioner's intentions. Might there be many meanings, or is there but one meaning? Does the question imply that the questioner has read the words and knows what the author intended? Is the text dealt with as though it were an object that, if severely worked upon, would yield its secrets, like DNA or a moon rock? Margaret Meek refers to this approach to reading as "one that treats the tale or book as simply a stimulus" (1982, p. 289). In this view, the teacher or examiner "owns" that stimulus and merely "rents it out" briefly to readers, with the reader holding little or no responsibility for the response.

When readers in schools read and respond, how they respond is influenced by the sense they have of who "owns" the text. In Readers' Workshops we believe that a literary work comes into being afresh while a reader is reading it. It comes into being *during* the reading, not after completion at some defined "snapshot" moment (Beach 1990, p. 65). When we as teachers understand this process we realize that we cannot own the meanings that our readers create during the reading. What we can do is to arrange for discussion group time for our students to talk about their emerging meanings. We can provide places for exploratory writing, whether in dialogue letters between classmates or between students and ourselves, or through response journals. We can also encourage further reflection on these meanings by questioning and sharing responses.

When reading is understood as a transaction between the reader and the text, it takes on the role of a conversation (Eeds and Wells 1989). The reader approaches the text with anticipation and wonderment. Questions and predictions drive the act of reading forward. The text, however, is "conversation frozen in time." The author is not present to answer the unanswerable or to explain the unfathomable, so the reader seeks clarification by "re-reading" the written text's cues. That is, readers take on an "ownership" of the text because they do the thinking and the making of meaning. Their involvement is a "hand-crafting" of that text's place in their lives, a personalizing of its meaning.

Students as builders: *risks and approximations*

> ...for all the reading research we have financed, we are certain only that good readers pick their own way to literacy in the company of

friends who encourage and sustain them and that...the enthusiasm of a trusted adult can make the difference.

—Margaret Meek (1982a, p. 193)

When we teachers "give up" traditional controls over talk and meaning-making, we become collaborative learners with our students. In all language situations where students and teachers are in collaboration, students' confidence and competence are built. The rights to be listened to — not spoken at — and to be encouraged — not dominated — are embedded in the principle of *risks and approximations.*

In order to empower students to take chances with meaning-making, we must create an atmosphere of trust in which students feel safe to risk "giving it a go." That right of the students to approximate — to estimate, to guess — by trying out new ideas, by thinking out loud and on paper about the texts they have read, is a certain and undeniable right in the supportive classroom.

Ralph Peterson and Maryann Eeds remind us that "...we concern ourselves with the *direction* of the responses children make to literature..." (1990, p. 23). Rather than holding the image of a single correct response, those of us teaching in Readers' Workshops consider the path of interpretation that our students are on, judging that path's potential to bring about progressively more complex and thoughtful responses to literature. We constantly use our workshops to encourage students to take risks in order to become better at approximating, to become better at negotiating the words that will reveal personal and communal meanings they have gained from their reading.

The principle of risks and approximations challenges us as teachers in agonizing ways. We have to watch constantly that we are not imposing our more experienced views onto our students' interpretations. We need to question students and draw them out. We need to give them time to explore their ideas until they form; and we need to accept that some ideas will not come to completion for some students. We are guided by a sense of what meanings may come from reading the stories, poems and books but we also have to react supportively to the tentative appearances of those meanings. We will be challenged by our students just as they are by us; our reactions should urge them forward, not shut them down. And, with all this, we must live with the uncertainty of not knowing exactly what methods will ensure that our students take risks and make approximations as they become increasingly confident and competent meaning-makers. How we handle problems in our workshops, how we show our comfort with not knowing all the answers, how we draw together everyone in the class to help build a sense of communal meaning-making will teach our students, and ourselves, to trust the process.

When we really "know" the risks and approximations principle, we will have our bridge to literacy half built. All four principles to this point support the idea of **meaning-making**: through *authenticity* of reading material, through *immersion* in the reading environment, through *shared responsibility* for making reading a *meaning-making* activity, and through the *risk-taking* setting that allows *approximations*.

Now we can look at the other principles that guide Readers' Workshops, principles that help us to think in practical terms about how we are assuring that our readers have strategies to make meaning so that they will be able to belong to the community of readers.

Stones held aloft: *demonstrations of reading*

...every reading and writing teacher should be a member of the [literacy] club. Many teachers are surprised when they reflect upon what they actually demonstrate to children about reading and writing during the school day.

—Frank Smith (1988, p. 12)

We teachers decide what our classrooms will be like: in doing so, we demonstrate the esteem we hold for reading. We give out messages by how much time we give for reading and how we react to response journals. Every event and every choice we make is guided by some assumption about learning to be a reader. Every action and every decision is a demonstration of what we think it is to be a reader.

Brian Cambourne writes that demonstrations are those "artifacts and actions from which we can learn" (1988, p. 47). There can be no principle more central to the teacher's role in Readers' Workshops than this principle of demonstration, for it points to the way of facilitating, of structuring, and of guiding readers to ownership of the reading process. When we model talking about books, share what we are reading and how it affects us, and read aloud from our own response journals, we aren't just showing off our literacy; we are providing our students with demonstrations of the "artifacts and actions of literacy" with which we happen to be familiar. How we reveal our caring about the impact of a novel upon an individual student lets all students know implicitly what literature is for. How we mould lessons to the needs of our students lets the students know explicitly how the reading task is accomplished. Our behaviour as teachers becomes purposeful and specific, structuring and controlling, yet it does so in a mindful, sharing, supportive way.

This principle of demonstration places demands upon our knowledge and understanding. We need to know what strategies readers may draw upon to make meaning, such as predicting, skimming, and inferring. We must understand how literature stimulates readers' imaginations, helps us understand ourselves, provides temporary diversion, or puts us into touch with others unlike ourselves.

Understanding the power of demonstrations also means knowing when and how to stay out of the way so that the results of demonstrations may take effect. Always being "helpful" does not always allow students to have a reason to reread or to stop to contemplate. Finally, while we are trying not to interfere, we can be observing, listening to and noting our students drawing upon the richness of the demonstrations around them. Students demonstrate *to one another* how to link literature to life or how to handle breakdowns in understanding. Everyone shares in demonstrating!

Cementing stones: from the personal to the communal — *communities of readers interpreting texts*

...reading involves social relationships among people: among teachers and students, among parents and children, and among authors and readers. The social relationships involved in reading include establishing social groups and ways of interacting with others; gaining or maintaining status and social position; and acquiring culturally appropriate ways of thinking, problem solving, valuing, and feeling.

—David Bloome (1985, p. 134)

Communities of readers

How is it that we often forget, when we plan our reading programs, that *we* read books recommended to us by people whose opinions we value? Why do we forget our own impulses to talk about a good read with someone? Adults naturally share their reading with their communities of reading friends. When we turn to look at young readers we find the same phenomena. They don't need to be told to make friends with someone else who owns Tintin books so they can share; they just do it.

We naturally tend to bring what is meaningful to us into a *community*, into connection with others. A powerful concept of the "literacy club" where "members [of the club] help newcomers to become experts" has been promoted by Frank Smith (1985, p. 125). Both reading and writing, done as part of meaningful actions, with expert help available, bring one into the "club" or community (1985, pp. 123–126).

Response groups

In classrooms, the community in action comes alive in the "response group." When readers have "grand conversations" about what they are reading rather than responding to the "gentle inquisitions" of comprehension questions, they are more likely to succeed in responding fully to literature (Harp 1989). Maryann Eeds and Deborah Wells (1989) found that in the course of "grand conversations" in their classrooms group members articulated their views, sometimes revised them in light of the discussion, shared relevant stories to make the literature personal, triggering identification in others, and participated actively as readers — predicting, confirming and evaluating. The presence of conversation and the group together permit this reflection and analysis of reading to occur. Community grows when people talk together about their reading.

Really believing in the community as an interpretive force can be difficult until we realize that teacher research in elementary classrooms confirms that "...literature response groups are powerful resources for learning through talk in the classroom" (Strickland et al. 1989, p. 196). Student-led reading conferences or response groups demonstrate reading comprehension in action and help students to "extend their literary awareness" (p. 200).

Dialogue

Sharing meaning-making in small group dialogues or in dialogue letters written between students or between students and teacher as they are reading offers additional opportunities for making better readers. When small group negotiation of authors' meanings and intentions occurs as a central and vital activity, the cooperative swapping of insights and opinions serves to stretch students into deeper discoveries. These discoveries go on to **empower** the students' deliberations and dialogues. "People in dialogue need each other.... Working together, partners in dialogue call one another forth as they seek to comprehend the world" (Peterson and Eeds 1990, p. 14).

Celebrations

> We are used to thinking of the text as the medium of communication
> between author and reader.... Perhaps we should consider the text as
> an even more general medium of communication among readers.
> —*Louise M. Rosenblatt (1978, p. 146)*

Celebrations are the bringing together of readers in a joyous exchange of views about books. Our students' responses to what they read are extended through celebrations that give them reasons to revisit the texts they have enjoyed, whether stories, plays, poems or novels. Whenever students are happy and excited about what they have read and want to share it, they are celebrating. Celebrations may look as simple as reading a favourite part of a story or a book to a discussion group or to a visiting parent in the classroom. They may involve dramatizing a section of a book or creating a diorama of the major setting. In practice, what celebrations do is give students cause to reread and, often, to reinterpret what they have read through other media: art, drama, scripting, explaining, retelling.

When a group of readers are moved to exhibit their understanding of a mystery novel by "selling" it to their classmates in a book talk, then a bonding of readers happens. The group works out how to share the story without revealing the mystery; their fellow classmates are invited to enjoy their own reading of the novel.

In classrooms that have visitors who ask students about their reading there are many opportunities for students to share the books they have happily read. The visiting administrator, parent or senior citizen — all will talk about books; they are not simply audiences for prepared speeches. Readers' Workshops exist when readers find themselves gossiping about books and recommending them to one another.

Transformed: The Arch as More than the Stones

> Virtually any product of complex learning can be reduced to component parts by logical analysis, for analytic logic is a powerful invention of the mind. But a fallacy occurs when the analysis is automatically assumed to be a blueprint of how the learning was achieved in the first place. This fallacy is often devastating for instruction....
>
> —*Anne M. Bussis et al. (1985, p. 4)*

Reducing Readers' Workshops to a blueprint is not the goal of the writers in this book. Indeed, the manner in which we implemented our own workshops varied greatly depending on our classroom experiences, our professional reading and support groups, our resources, our curricular demands, and the characteristics of our particular students. Yet all our workshops reflected in some way the foundational principles I have discussed above.

To a person, the teacher-writers in this book agree that each teacher will need to build his or her own Readers' Workshop bridge from literature to literacy. At the beginning of this chapter I talked about the foundational principles as the stones for the bridge; they are each teacher's materials. I looked at the arch of the bridge as the direction or purpose of Readers' Workshops; it is that which leads to "...a community of active, independent, self-reliant readers, making meaning from texts, resisting manipulation and mind control, preserving literacy and liberty" (*English Journal*, January 1988, p. 31)

Becoming your own bridge builder means that you, Marco Polo-like, examine carefully the craftsmanship of the stones and then allow yourself to get caught up in the pleasure of using your well-crafted stones to form strong and smooth arches. Stones and arch work together; it is as though they are transformed into more than one or the other. And you, the builder, find that you have been transformed; your teaching practices have been transformed; your own reading is transformed. You will have found the shape of your arch.

Without stones there is no arch.

# References

Beach, Richard. 1990. "New Directions in Research on Response to Literature." In Farrell, Edmund & James R. Squire, Ed. *Transactions with Literature*. Urbana, IL: National Council of Teachers of English.

Bloome, David. 1985. "Reading as Social Process."*Language Arts*. 62, 134–142.

Bruner, Jerome. 1986. *Actual Minds, Possible Worlds*. Cambridge, MA.: Harvard University Press.

Bussis, Anne M. et al. 1985. *Inquiry into Meaning: An Investigation of Learning to Read*. Hillsdale, NJ: Lawrence Erlbaum Associates.

Calvino, Italo. 1972. *Invisible Cities*. New York, NY: Harvest/Harcourt Brace Jovanovich Inc.

Cambourne, Brian. 1988. *The Whole Story*. Auckland, NZ: Ashton Scholastic.

Eeds, Maryann & Deborah Wells. 1989. "Grand Conversations: An Exploration of Meaning Construction in Literature Study Groups." *Research in the Teaching of English*. 23, 4–28.

Emig, Janet. 1990. "Our Missing Theory." In Moran, Charles & Elizabeth F. Penfield, Ed. *Conversations: Contemporary Critical Theory and the Teaching of Literature*. Urbana, IL: National Council of Teachers of English.

English Journal. 1981. Urbana, IL: National Council of Teachers of English. January, 31.

Harp, Bill. 1989. "Why don't you ask comprehension questions?" *The Reading Teacher*. 42, 638–639.

Huck, Charlotte. 1987. "Literature as the Content of Reading." *Theory into Practice*. XXVI, Special Issue, 374–382.

Meek, Margaret. 1982. "What Counts as Evidence in Theories of Children's Literature." *Theory into Practice*. XXI, 184–292.

Meek, Margaret. 1982a. *Learning to Read*. London, Eng.: The Bodley Head.

Peterson, Ralph & Maryann Eeds. 1990. *Grand Conversations: Literature Groups in Action*. Richmond Hill, ON: Scholastic Canada Ltd.

Rosenblatt, Louise M. 1990. "Retrospect." In Farrell, Edmund & James R. Squire, Ed. *Transactions with Literature: A Fifty-Year Perspective*. Urbana, IL: National Council of Teachers of English.

Rosenblatt, Louise M. 1989. "Writing and Reading: The Transactional Theory." In Mason, Jana M., Ed. *Reading and Writing Connections*. Boston, MA: Allyn & Bacon Inc.

Rosenblatt, Louise M. 1983. "The Reading Transaction: What For?" In Parker, R. & F. Davis, Ed. *Developing Literacy: Young Children's Use of Language*. Newark, DE: International Reading Association.

Rosenblatt, Louise M. 1978. *The Reader, the Text, the Poem: The Transactional Theory of the Literary Work*. Carbondale, IL: Southern Illinois University Press.

Smith, Frank. 1988. *Joining the Literacy Club*. Portsmouth, NH: Heinemann Educational Books, Inc.

Smith, Frank. 1985. *Reading Without Nonsense*. Second edition. New York, NY: Teachers College Press.

Strickland, Dorothy S., Rose Marie Dillon, Leslie Funkhouser, Mary Glick, & Corrine Rogers. 1989. "Research Currents: Classroom Dialogue During Literature Response Groups." *Language Arts*. 66, 192–200.

Vygotsky, L. S. 1978. *Mind in Society*. Cambridge, MA: Harvard University Press.

Fostering a Community of Readers with Readers' Workshops

Blanche Lamont has provided direction to teachers and administrators in the development of Readers' Workshop approaches during her tenure as language arts consultant with the Calgary Board of Education and as coordinator of the Calgary Writing Project, a staff development project of the Calgary Board of Education. She has eighteen years of teaching and consulting experience. She draws largely upon her grades four through six teaching and her in-service work with teachers for this piece in which she outlines a possible model for an open-ended conception of Readers' Workshops. Ms. Lamont continues to work with others in study groups on reading-writing connections, and to make presentations at schools, conferences, and in-service workshops.

When my colleagues and I come together at workshops and in study groups to share our experiences with Readers' Workshops, we eat, drink and talk... and talk! Yes, we do like to talk, but the reality is that we *need* to talk. Through this talk we strengthen our common goals and celebrate our differences. We recognize that each of us brings our own experiences and interests to our classrooms and that our students bring their own unique experiences and interests too. There is no teacher's guide with step-by-step lesson plans for Readers' Workshops, and we don't want one. We understand that a Readers' Workshop looks different in each classroom and that's the way it should be.

But those of us who teach in Readers' Workshops do share certain common beliefs and goals. We believe that our students will become better readers by doing a lot of reading, that reading is a valuable lifelong activity, and that literature enriches our lives and our students' lives. Our goal is to foster a community atmosphere in which reading is important, where teachers and students behave like "real" readers.

How do "real" readers behave? First of all, they make their own choices about what they will read. Then they spend a lot of time reading. They also love to talk about books, and to make recommendations about good books to others. Simply put, a Readers' Workshop is a vehicle for allowing our

students the opportunity to do these things. It is one way that we can foster a community of readers in our classrooms in which everyone, including the teacher, is a reader.

Fostering a community of readers cannot be accomplished with fifteen minutes of daily silent reading squeezed into a busy timetable. If we want our students to become readers, then we must allow them time to choose what they will read and then give them time to read and to discuss their books. One way to find this time is to make Readers' Workshop a unit or theme that is alternated with other units in the reading program. Or Readers' Workshop can be made the entire reading program for the year.

Through all our talking, my colleagues and I seem to come back again and again to some basic elements that are common to all our Readers' Workshops. I want to give an overview of these elements for you to consider when planning for your own Readers' Workshops. Not all these elements will be included in one day nor even in one week. While my own experiences have been with elementary students, the elements I discuss below are equally applicable to Readers' Workshops in secondary schools.

Planning the Environment — Variety and Flexibility

Forming Small Groups

The classroom community is strengthened when students work in small groups. In small groups the connections the students make through their shared experiences with a book can be enhanced. Working in small groups also helps students to realize that more than one viewpoint can be considered when interpreting a story. (It should be remembered, however, that it is natural for students to want to read a book alone sometimes. Those students reading on their own can still join together for discussion about their books with other students.)

Below are some suggestions for forming groups.

- In my classes, I try to be sure that there are multiple copies of as many different books as possible and I make sure these books are available through the library or within the classroom. Three or four copies of each title seem to work well. Groups of three or four students cooperate to choose books that they will read together during school time as well as at home. You may want to place students in groups initially, but you can expect that your students will soon begin to form their own groups. The advantage of allowing students to group themselves before choosing a book is that the group will likely stay together longer and read several books together.

- Another way to encourage groupings is to have about seven to ten titles available (three to four copies of each title) and then do book talks to introduce each of the books (see "Suggested Mini-lessons, Section F," below). After the book talks, each student chooses which book he or she wants to read and joins the group reading that book. This method works well if there is a time limit on the book to be read. It does not work as well when the students are going to read more than one book. Each group tends to finish books at different rates and re-grouping to read another book can be difficult unless all groups finish their books at the same time.

- If multiple copies of books in the same genre or on the same topic can be put together (e.g., books on horses, dogs, science fiction, historical fiction, mystery or versions of the same fairy tale), then groups may be formed according to the genres or topics. In this case, students in a group usually read different titles rather than the same title.

Time for Reading

Students need time to read their books together or alone, in whichever way they choose. If a group of students is reading the same book, then the students can also negotiate among themselves how much reading they will do at home. (It is important the students understand that if they are reading the same book they should all read together to get to the same points in the book at the same time. If one or two read ahead in the book, the group discussion will not work as well.)

If the children are very young, you might read the book to the small group.

Time for Discussion/Conferencing

I encourage my students to discuss their books in small groups. The discussions may be held at any time — before, during or after reading. The students sometimes use their reading response journals (see next section) as a way to begin discussion or they may simply list the things they want to discuss and bring their lists to the group. It is important that we, as teachers, be involved in these ongoing conversations and that we not confine our participation to discussions after a book is finished. During these sessions we should truly try to be a member of the group, not the leader. To do this we need to discourage students from directing their comments to us. We need instead to encourage them to value their own insights and to share these insights with their classmates — and with us, too, as interested readers.

Discussion or conferencing times provide us with opportunities to teach students how to respond directly to comments made by another student rather than just telling their own reactions. We can also guide students towards a more complex understanding of the book during these sessions.

NOTE: Students may need help to learn how to talk about their reading. The "Suggested Mini-lessons, Section D" below provide some suggestions for mini-lessons that focus on discussion skills.

Time for Writing: Reading Response Journals

I have my students keep reading response journals (also sometimes called literature logs or lit. logs) in which they respond to the books they are reading. A section of the journal can be used to record titles, authors, and quick comments about the books that have been read. Lead-ins such as "I wonder…," "I don't like…," etc., can be helpful to students.

Reading response journals can be used in a variety of ways. Some secondary teachers use response journals primarily as literature logs; other teachers use the journals as "dialogue" journals in which they have their students write "letters" about their readings to one another and/or to the teacher. Often in this use of the journal students will trade their journals back and forth, writing responses to the letters other students have written to them in those students' logs. Using reading response journals as dialogue journals works especially well when your students are reading different titles. Any variation in the use of response journals is possible — as long as the journal serves to stimulate response and discussion while giving students the opportunity for recording first thoughts and reflections about their reading. (See "Suggested Mini-lessons, Section C," for more detail on using reading response journals.)

When I respond to the students' entries in their journals I try to help stimulate the students' thinking about literature. The response journals can also serve as catalysts for large and small group discussions if students begin discussion groups by sharing their responses. The response journals also give me valuable insights about my students as readers, such as what they are understanding, what they like to read, and how they relate what they read to their own lives.

NOTE: Students may need help in learning how to express their personal reactions. Mini-lessons that focus on response journals can be planned. See "Suggested Mini-lessons, Section C."

Readers' Workshops in Action

Keeping Track

Once students are reading alone or in groups, deciding when to read, discuss and write, and possibly moving on to new books, I find I develop a number of ways to monitor what is going on. You may develop your own checklists to record what Nancy Atwell has called the "status-of-the-class" each day—who's reading, who's tape-recording discussions, who's preparing to share their books, and so on. Using checklists in this way is one way to check up on which groups or individuals need your attention once a mini-lesson is over. Groups may invite you to help them with a problem or may indicate they have a recording of a discussion for you to listen to.

Reading and responding to students' response journals, keeping anecdotal records of students' book-sharing projects, maintaining a running record of your own mini-lessons, and just "touching base" with each group during its reading/writing/discussing times are all ways to track what students are doing each day.

Assessment-in-Action

There are many ways of assessing students participating in Readers' Workshops. Most teachers continue to use methods and tools that they have developed for assessing growth and progress in other literature-based activities. But one of the strategies I have found most effective has been to determine what assessment questions I want answered; my observations and anecdotal records then seem to develop easily for the questions.

Some of the questions I think about are

- What are my students' attitudes towards reading? Are they willing to read intensively? Are they changing? How?
- Are they becoming more confident?
- Are they challenging themselves in reading? In difficulty levels? In length?
- Are they reading a variety of genres?
- Does their joy in some literature show in how they talk and write?
- Are they reading in greater depth? Are they more involved and engaged?
- Do their conferences and reading journals show personal involvement? Are they relating what they have read to their personal lives? Are they expressing strong feelings about issues and events in their books? Do they give opinions about the characters' actions and statements?
- Are they reading more? Is the volume of reading increasing? Number of pages or books? Amount of time spent in the act of reading?
- Do they go beyond plot summaries in conversation or in writing?
- Are they quoting from their books or referring to parts in them?
- Are they willing to share their thinking? Their reading? Their books? Do they gossip about books and recommend them to one another?
- Do they take up suggestions from others?
- What connections seem to be showing up between their reading and their own writing? Are ideas flowing back and forth? Are they discussing their own writing differently?
- How are they talking and listening in their response groups?
- Does their learning seem to be purposeful? Are they caught up in the Workshop? Do they seem to have their own goals? Are they motivated to read outside of class?
- What reading strategies are they using? Are they reading for meaning? Are they making pictures in their heads, making predictions, summarizing events, and so on? How are they handling difficulties (word recognition and lack of comprehension or miscomprehension) as they read?

and most important

- Are they beginning to evaluate their own reading by asking themselves the same kinds of questions as these?

Sometimes colleagues and I ask questions about more mundane issues such as: Are the students keeping a reading list of books completed? Are they writing regularly in their journals? Are they completing some sort of after-reading project? When we ask these questions, we need also to ask ourselves whether we are confusing quantity for quality.

When do I think about the more important questions? Usually while in the midst of everything — during mini-lessons, when I listen in on groups in discussion, while students are reading to me, during celebrations, in other words, whenever it is possible to be a "kid watcher."

Some of my colleagues have devised informal checklists of their own covering some of the items in my questions. At junior high level there tends to be more student self-evaluation on some of the points. Usually such tools are used for a while and then put away once the teacher is comfortable with what he or she is looking for. The biggest challenge is to keep a range of written records of what you have observed.

For gathering marks when that is required, some colleagues have set up point scales; however, these seem to me to betray the intentions of Readers' Workshops so I feel that I can't recommend them.

Time for Instruction — Direct and Indirect

After I have organized the resources and set up the basic structure for a Readers' Workshop in my classroom, I take a little side-step and let the students take control of the workshop, for at this time our main role as teachers becomes one of guide, facilitator and cheerleader. But there is also a place for direct instruction. As guides we watch our students and converse with them to see where they lead us, to see where they need to grow. As we watch and talk with our students, we develop mini-lessons. Some mini-lessons may be quite lengthy; some may last five minutes. Some lessons may be presented to the whole class, but much of our teaching is done with individuals or with small groups during reading conferences.

Possible Types of Mini-lessons

Attitudes	Procedures
- why read for pleasure	- modelling how to discuss books
- finding time to read	- modelling for reading response
- collecting books	journals
- borrowing books	- where materials are kept
	- other organization issues

Literature	Strategy/Skill
- focus on authors and illustrators	- choosing books
- poetry	- what to do when you don't know
- different genres	a word
- story structure	- making inferences
- sharing books (by teachers	- monitoring — does it make sense?
and by students)	

The section "Suggested Mini-lessons" on pages 32–42 gives *suggestions* for more detailed lessons.

Time for Celebrating Books

The process of students recommending books to other students needs to be part of the classroom reading community. The students can prepare many kinds of projects about their books to present to their classmates or they can learn to do effective book talks. There are suggestions for ways to celebrate and share books in the "Suggested Mini-lessons" and in the "Examples of Book-sharing Projects for Students" at the end of this article, but you already probably have files full of ideas!

Time for Reading Daily to Our Students

In elementary school, the daily storytime is an ideal opportunity for us to broaden our students' world of literature. I often introduce a new author to my students by reading one of his or her books, or I might read the first book in a series. I am careful also to choose books that are a little too difficult for most of my students to read on their own, as well as books from different genres, including poetry, so that the students experience all kinds of literature.

This storytime allows us to reinforce reading strategies such as predicting, questioning and confirming (see "Suggested Mini-lessons, Section H"). I also stop occasionally to discuss elements of a story, the way characters are developed, some particularly powerful description, or how the author uses language to evoke emotions or excitement (see "Suggested Mini-lessons, Section E"). Some of the best short mini-lessons can be presented during storytime.

You Are a Role Model

Our students need to see that we are readers. We can achieve this goal by telling them about our own reading interests and habits, where and when we read, where we get our books. Sometimes we might sit and read when our students are reading. We also read books that our students are reading. When we ourselves read and enjoy the books in our school libraries, we can make recommendations to our students on a daily basis and can significantly influence and extend their reading. A community atmosphere really develops when our students begin to make recommendations to us and we read the books they recommend.

Some Suggested Mini-lessons for Readers' Workshops

The following "lessons" are only a few examples of the many kinds of instruction you can plan for your Readers' Workshops. The suggestions are meant *as possible starting points only*. Many of the topics suggested here can be presented to the whole class or can be discussed informally with individuals or with small groups.

Many of the ideas underpinning these lessons have been developed from ideas in other publications, or have been collected at workshops and study group meetings. I would like, therefore, to thank those who have pioneered in writing in the field and to thank as well all my colleagues for sharing their expertise with me for this collection.

A. Attitudes

1. Book Collections
Discuss
- how we develop a book collection
- how to organize our books, where to keep them
- the pleasures of having a book collection
- the pleasures of browsing through a bookstore

2. Borrowing Books
Discuss
- how to get a public library card
- using the library
- the pleasures of being in a library and browsing through books
- borrowing books from friends

3. Why Read?
Discuss and list answers on chart paper
- why do people read? (for example: for pleasure, for adventure, to learn, to find out about different people, places, times, to help us personally, etc.)

4. How Do We Find Time To Read?
Discuss
- when people read
- how they find time to read during the day
- where people read
- the cozy aspects of curling up with a good book

NOTE: We need to be a model — discuss the reading we do, where we read and how often we read.

5. Why Don't People Read?

Discuss

- why some people don't read very much (for example: too busy, not good at it)
- why reading can be such a pleasure
- how we grow as readers by reading
- if you're not good at it — how you can get better

6. Thickness of Books

Discuss

- does the thickness of a book indicate its difficulty? Show examples of thin books that are difficult and thick books that are easy to read.

B. Choosing Books

1. What Attracts Us to a Book?

Discuss and show

- covers of books
- sometimes unattractive covers can be misleading; show students examples
- show examples of books that have different covers because they have been published by different publishers or have been printed at different times; compare these covers and discuss why the covers may have been changed (for example: to make the cover more exciting; to make it look more modern; to make the cover "fit" the "style" of a series of books, etc.)

2. Using Special Features of a Book

Discuss reviews, story synopses and chapter headings

- how we read the back of a book or the inside flaps of a book jacket to see what the book is about
- how reading reviews on the back cover or inside flaps of a book cover can help us
- how we can use chapter headings

3. Choosing Easy, Medium, Challenging Books

Discuss

- how it's okay to choose an easy book, but how we should try a challenging book sometimes
- discuss the five-finger method for choosing books so the books won't be too hard (Read a few pages of a book — if there are usually more than five words on each page that are unfamiliar, the book will be a challenge.)

- a section of the response journal can be used as a reading record where students can rate the books they read as Easy, Medium, or Challenging

4. Different Genres

Discuss and list
- different genres — science fiction, realistic fiction, fantasy, historical fiction, mystery, etc.

Explain each genre
- encourage students to read in different genres
- in small groups have the students discuss books in each category

5. Different Genres (several lessons)

Present book talks that focus on a different genre for each lesson. When possible use books or stories the students have read.

C. Response Journals

1. Whole-class Response

- drawing from a story that is being read aloud or read by the whole class, develop a class response to the reading and write the response(s) on the board or on chart paper. Emphasize personal reactions, criticisms, predictions, asking questions, etc. Re-emphasize that response journals are for entering thoughts and feelings and questions about what is being read, not for retelling the story.

2. You as a Model

- you write a response to the novel being read by the whole class. Read your response to the class and discuss its main points — predictions, questions, personal reactions. In small groups, students discuss what to include in a response journal.

3. Using Students' Response Journals

- with the students' permission, choose sentences or paragraphs from various response journals to read aloud as examples for the class
- discuss why the examples you have chosen are effective responses

4. Lead-ins

List on chart paper or on a small sheet of paper that can be glued into each student's response journal some possible lead-ins that might help the students get started when they are writing in their journals:

- I wonder...
- I think...
- I like...

- I wish...
- I don't understand...
- If I were the author...

- This part reminds me...
- I predict...
- It seems to me...
- I question...

D. Discussion of Books

1. Discussing Books — Modelling
- find other adults — librarian, principal, resource teacher, etc. — to model a book discussion
- begin reading a short story — stop for discussion — model a poor discussion (for example, no eye contact, no responding to one another, interrupting one another, not showing respect for another's opinions, etc.)
- continue reading — model a good discussion
- students critique the discussions

2. Taping Discussions
- have groups tape their discussions when possible
- listen to the tapes and choose a fairly successful one
- with the group's permission, play the tape for the class
- critique what happened
- discuss what makes a good discussion

3. Modelling "Piggy-backing"
- choose a small group to demonstrate "piggy-backing" for the class
- begin reading a short story and stop
- the group begins a discussion — you direct students to respond to one another's comments by "piggy-backing" on one another's comments
- discuss piggy-backing as a discussion technique

4. Who Makes the Rules?
- have each reading group make their own rules for discussion; someone records
- each group shares its rules with the whole class

5. Post-its
- give each group a package of small Post-its
- each student marks the passages he/she wants to bring into the discussion

6. Using Student Response Journals
- before discussing the books they are reading, each student in the small group reads his/her last response journal entry to the rest of the group as a stimulus for discussion

E. Story Elements

1. Plot Graph
- demonstrate a plot graph using a short story that is familiar to your students to show how excitement builds and then plateaus

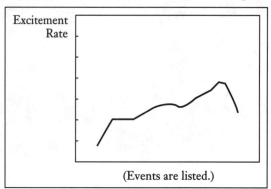

- students create plot graphs for the books they are reading

2. Conflict
- demonstrating with short stories or novels that all members of the class have read, discuss how almost every story has a conflict — either internal or external, or both

- students discuss, in small groups, the conflicts in the books they are reading; they decide whether the conflict is internal or external or both

3. Settings
- using books or stories that the class has read together, discuss how settings in books add to interest and help us to learn about different places and other times
- in groups of two or three, students discuss books they have read with settings that were interesting (different places or times); they discuss why they found the settings interesting and why some students found some settings interesting while others didn't.

4. Point of View
- using books or stories that are familiar to the whole class show how authors write from the third person and from the first person and discuss why (for example: Third person — can move between events and settings with several characters; First person — more personal reactions)

5. The Underlying Message
- explain how authors often want to give a special message in a book — they don't just tell the surface story, but try to make us think about bigger issues
- use stories and examples that are familiar to the whole class
- students try to think of what the authors are really trying to say in the books they are reading

6. Characters in Books
- in groups of two or three, students discuss two or three books they have read in terms of characters. Which characters are realistic? Which are stereotypical? Students discuss why they find some characters realistic, others stereotypical
- each group reports to the class; you point out how authors make characters real — with thoughts and feelings and internal conflict

7. Character/Proof
- demonstrate the following chart using a story that everyone has read:

What Character Is Like	Proof (from the text)

- students make a "character/proof" chart in their response journals using a character from a book they are reading and completing the chart by finding proof in the chapter they are reading

8. How Characters Change and Grow
- discuss novels or short stories that the class has read together in terms of how characters change and grow
- students, in groups of two or three, discuss characters in books they have read—how the characters changed or grew, what they learned about themselves, and how their attitudes changed

9. How Authors Develop Characters
- while reading a short story or novel to the class, stop occasionally to draw out how the author is making a character "real," such as by giving the character problems, showing how the character is not perfect, giving details of how the person is speaking and what he or she is doing, and/or sharing that character's feelings or thoughts
- discuss together how an author shows that the character is changing throughout the story or novel

F. Focus on Authors

1. Lives of Authors (several lessons)
- locate films and/or filmstrips and books about authors and their lives to use for discussions. Your teacher-librarian can be an important resource for you.

2. Book Talks
- present book talks on several books by the same author
- discuss the type(s) of books written by that author (for example: Roald Dahl, Jean Little)

3. Favourite Authors
- begin a Favourite Authors' chart with your students

- students nominate a favourite author and collect signatures from classmates
- students present book talks on some of that author's books to the class

G. Poetry

1. Teacher "Read Alouds"
- read poetry regularly to the class
- students respond to the poetry in small group discussions
- each group shares its response with the class

2. Student "Read Alouds"
- students practise poems to read aloud to the rest of the class
- students explain why they chose a particular poem
- other students respond to the poems that have been read aloud

3. Small Group "Read Alouds" (several lessons)
- each student chooses and prepares a poem to read
- each student reads his or her poem to a small group and receives response from the group
- each group decides what poem it would like to share with the whole class

H. Reading Strategies

1. What Are Reading Strategies?
- discuss what a "reading strategy" is; some strategies to talk about— using background knowledge, questioning, predicting, confirming, using context to figure out unknown words
- as a class, begin a web of reading strategies — discuss each
- ask students to give examples of how they have used strategies in their reading

2. Questioning, Predicting
- discuss the strategies of questioning and predicting — draw out how they help us with our reading
- read through a short story emphasizing and practising these strategies
- discuss how and where these strategies can be used when students are reading on their own

3. Making Predictions
- when beginning a novel or short story, read a few pages, then have students complete the following chart:

I Wonder	I Think

- encourage your students to confirm their predictions or to rethink them if they were wrong
- discuss again what a reading strategy is; encourage your students to think about questioning and predicting in all their reading

4. Making Inferences

- select a short story or short passage that requires students to make inferences in order to gain more meaning
- begin reading the story or passage together. Stop and ask questions that require the students to make inferences. Then ask: "How did you know the answer to that question?" Students explain how they got the answers
- explain what inferring means — that not all information is written down, we have to "read between the lines," we are figuring out "invisible messages"
- continue reading and stopping. Students work in small groups to show how they are making inferences
- encourage your students to generalize this strategy to all their reading (to look always for possible "invisible messages")

5. Background Knowledge

- find a short text that is ambiguous and make an overhead of it
- show the overhead — in small groups, students read and discuss what is happening in the story
- large group discussion — draw out how your students were able to make sense of the text because they used their background knowledge to make inferences
- remind the students to generalize using background knowledge to all their reading

6. Being Aware of Punctuation

- put a short passage on an overhead
- read the passage out loud without paying any attention to punctuation read the passage out loud paying attention to the punctuation; show

FOSTERING A COMMUNITY OF READERS

how it is easier to understand the passage when you pay attention to the punctuation than it is when you ignore the punctuation; show the students how to use punctuation in their own writing — periods, commas, quotation marks, etc. — to help make meaning clearer

7. Unfamiliar Words — What To Do (small group is probably best)
- put a "cloze" passage on an overhead — some of the larger words could be blanked out with only the first letter left
- demonstrate that using context clues is the most effective strategy to use when we meet an unfamiliar word
- discuss how to use context for clues to meaning — help your students generalize using context clues to their own reading

8. Unfamiliar Words — It's Okay To Skip Over Them
- discuss how you can skip over words occasionally (especially if they're names or places) and still retain meaning
- point out to your students that they must always monitor their reading. If they are skipping words so much that they are losing meaning, the text is too challenging. They should always ask themselves, "Does this make sense to me?"

9. Unfamiliar Words — Structural Analysis
- select a passage with words that have prefixes and suffixes
- students try to figure out the words using context clues FIRST
- then show students how these words can be recognized through the root words — explain prefixes and suffixes. Encourage students to use context clues to try to discover meaning FIRST!

I. Celebrating Books

1. Brainstorming Ideas
- ask your students to brainstorm ideas for ways of sharing books; discuss their ideas
- list the students' ideas on chart paper
- keep the list available for students to use

2. What Makes a Good Book Talk?
- demonstrate an effective book talk (ask your teacher-librarian to get involved)
- discuss and list what made the book talk effective
- encourage students to refer to this list when preparing their own book talks

3. Plan a Party

- have your students plan a celebration with food and refreshments
- plan how books can be celebrated at this special event

4. Performances

- students choose a Readers' Theatre script or short book to present to a group of younger students
- the students must advertise their performance via posters and P.A. announcements

5. Graffiti Board

- cover a bulletin board with paper and allow your students to write short messages about books and authors

Examples of Book-sharing Projects for Students

- Bring a small box from home to make a diorama of a scene from your book. You may use any materials that you can think of: Plasticine, construction paper, popsicle sticks, etc.
- Write a book review with an illustration for your book. You may contribute your review to a class book to be placed in your class library.

- Make a filmstrip showing what you think are the main events in your book. Be ready to tell the class about the book. Ask your teacher for the materials you will need to make your filmstrip.
- Write down what you think your book would say about itself if it could talk.
- Write an interview between a magazine reporter and the author of the book or a character in the book you are reading, or write an interview between the author of the book and a character in the book.
- Make a puppet(s) to help you dramatize an event in your book or to introduce some characters to the class.
- Act out or make a play of an exciting part of your book. Present your play to the class.
- Take characters from more than one book to create a play for the class.
- Dress up as your favourite book character for the day.
- As a character in your book, write to the author complaining or thanking him/her about your part in the book.
- What would happen if a character from one book found himself/herself in another book? Write or act out this new situation.
- Make a colourful poster that illustrates some exciting parts of your book.
- Draw pictures on overhead transparencies to go along with a book talk about your book. See the teacher about providing you with overhead transparencies and showing you how to use them.
- Make a Plasticine model of a character(s) in your book.
- Make a soap carving of a character in your book.

References

Atwell, Nancie. 1987. *In the Middle: Writing, Reading, and Learning with Adolescents*. Portsmouth, NH: Boynton/Cook Publishers Inc.

Calkins, Lucy. 1986. *The Art of Teaching Writing*. Portsmouth, NH: Heinemann Educational Books, Inc.

Hansen, Jane. 1987. *When Writers Read*. Portsmouth, NH: Heinemann Educational Books, Inc.

Harste, Jerome, Cathy Short, Carolyn Burke. 1988. *Creating Classrooms for Authors: The Reading-Writing Connection*. Portsmouth, NH: Heinemann Educational Books, Inc.

Looking in on the Readers' Workshop

*As well as having taught grades one through six, **Barbara C. Wallace** has been a resource teacher and an elementary school vice-principal. She has completed a year as an educational consultant with Alberta's provincial education department, returning to her role as supervisor of curriculum for a predominantly rural school division. Ms. Wallace is also a member of a team authoring a primary program in language arts.*

How would you like to go on an adventure and have no one with whom to share the wonders and/or disappointments? If, like Emily Dickinson and me, you believe, "There is no frigate like a book to take us lands away," then you realize the irony of asking students to read and then never providing that opportunity for them to share and really enjoy the adventure.

As I observed teachers and students at work in classrooms in my role as curriculum supervisor, and as I reflected on Emily Dickinson's view of reading, I saw the need to ask questions that would cause teachers to revisit their beliefs about the way children learn to read. One of the questions that kept emerging was, "What do we want students to learn?" Another question closely related to that was, "How do we as teachers see our role in that learning process?"

If students learn what we teach, then we must model appropriate behaviours and strategies. Teachers who believe that text in and of itself contains meaning see their role as one of directing students to the text to get answers to questions of the "what" and "who" nature. Their students tend to read only to seek information.

On the other hand, if teachers see meaning as being created by the reader as he or she becomes actively engaged in the reading process then they will provide students with opportunities to live through text. In such situations, readers can reflect on what they are experiencing as they engage in the text. Questions of much different nature begin to be asked — "What do you think?" "How do you feel?" "What was there in the text that contributed to that feeling or to that thought?" Teachers who endorse this approach see their role very differently than do teachers who see the text itself as containing the meaning. They see themselves as facilitators or coaches. The questions they pose and their own responses to their students' questions are for these teachers key strategies for taking the students beyond the text. These teachers provide opportunities for students to respond to text in different modes. They engage in dialogue with their students in conference situations and/or through dialogue journals or letters.

These teachers argue that since children, like adults, bring varied experiences to print, two children reading the same book will have different insights. Imagine the excitement when Sarah realizes that Sherene has a different interpretation of the text but that they are both right! The realization that the words on the page are really only part of the story is the beginning of an understanding of what reading is all about. Students will understand that reading is a transaction between themselves and the text they are reading. Students not only understand that what they bring to print is important but that the text offers them something to respond to as well.

Those teachers who have involved their students in Writers' Workshops see Readers' Workshops as a logical step, a way of nurturing the connection between reading and writing. For those students who have experience in Writers' Workshops, the transition to Readers' Workshops is relatively easy. It is an opportunity for them to take control of their reading the way they have taken control of their writing. For students who have not been involved in Writers' Workshops, it is just a matter of time before they too become completely immersed in the type of "book sharing" that is so typical of Readers' Workshops. With delight I have observed teachers enthusiastically guiding their students into a community of readers. Even more rewarding and pleasurable have been the opportunities to share in the excitement generated by the members of those communities.

I listened with amazement as a group of grade five students discussed a question brought to the group by one of its members. Susan had been most annoyed by what she saw as the author's unfair treatment of a character who had, until that point, not endeared himself to anyone. Her question, "Why does the author always make the bad guy lose?", got an immediate response. Listen to her classmates discuss:

> "Well, when authors write they teach us a lesson. If a bad character wins then we'll think that it's okay to do what he did."
>
> "Yes, but he doesn't always have to win. Sometimes even bad characters can do good things and I think the author should make him feel good. How would you like it if nobody ever said you did something right?"
>
> "I don't think they should say so, if I don't do anything right."
>
> "But you are forgetting that David has done something right."

Another member of the group finally gets a chance to speak.

> "You said that authors write to teach us lessons but that's only in fables.
> This story we're talking about is not a fable."

And so the discussion continued. I eventually got a turn so I asked, "How would you, as an author, deal with a situation such as this in your own writing?"

> "I have read books," said Corey, "where the author sometimes makes you think one character won and then at the end you find out that he didn't really win. Maybe that's what Susan means. That would work, wouldn't it Susan?"
>
> "Yeah, something like that would be fairer, I think," said Susan, somewhat relieved.
>
> "Not only that but it makes the story more interesting," Corey continued.

A teacher would probably not have asked the question Susan asked. Certainly it would not have been included in a workbook that encourages the reader to seek answers from the text. While addressing a real concern expressed by a member of their community these students were able to make connections with other authors and with their own experiences.

Readers' Workshops afford learners forums for discussion and thereby with opportunities to gain a deeper understanding of what is being read. I am reminded of what Donald Graves wrote in *Discover Your Own Literacy*: "When children can share their reading of wonderful books, they encounter many minds: the teacher's, other children's, the author's and their own. Each provides space for the thinking of others" (p. 40). As a mature reader, I often find it useful to share what I am reading with a friend or a colleague, sometimes because I find it insightful or interesting to do so but, quite often, because I want to get someone else's point of view. In the supportive environment of Readers' Workshops, students feel equally free to share their views and seek out the opinions of others. They see themselves as part of a literate community where people read and talk about books.

As teachers in these communities observe and interact with their students they begin to reflect further on the question of what we want students to learn and our role in the process. The learning that is occurring becomes evident as they see students who are really empowered to come to new understandings from their reading, students who are not afraid to take risks by voicing their opinions and insights. They see competent, confident, self-directed learners whose writing is being enhanced by the work of other authors. Such outcomes provide teachers with clear indications of what students can learn and how Readers' Workshops may contribute to the process.

And how do students feel about Readers' Workshops? One only needs to listen to the deafening "Ah…" of disappointment that emanates from the classroom when the teacher says, "It's time to wind down for today." For me the answer is obvious.

## References

Dickinson, Emily. 1960. *Complete Poems*. Boston, MA: Little, Brown & Co. Inc.

Graves, Donald H. 1990. *Discover Your Own Literacy* in *The Reading/Writing Teacher's Companion Series*. Toronto, ON: Irwin Publishing.

Readers' Workshop from the Inside Out

Myrna Reeves comes to her role as Consultant for School Library Programs from classroom teaching and twelve years as a teacher-librarian where she was able to work on cooperative planning and teaching with other elementary teachers. She has helped teachers to begin with Readers' Workshops while assisting others to expand their effectiveness with workshops. Ms. Reeves presents at local, national and international conferences.

"Could you really believe a mother would react to her daughter's phone call that way?"

"Well, she was under a lot of pressure. With her job and being a single parent."

"What did you think about the ending? I found it kind of depressing."

"Really? Not me. I think those two will make it; they're survivors. Look at that last page..."

A group of students discussing the latest novel in their Readers' Workshop? Actually, it's a study group of teacher-librarians in the middle of a "grand conversation" about a book they have all read. This intensive dialogue was part of a process we engaged in in order to gain a deeper understanding of what a Readers' Workshop actually feels like, how it actually works for the students participating in it.

Our group was looking at various methods of involving students with literature. Some of us had already studied the philosophy supporting Readers' Workshops; others had worked with classroom teachers in the implementation of a workshop. But none of us had personally experienced the processes experienced by students reading in a workshop setting.

In order to understand the processes our students might experience, we agreed to read a children's novel none of us was familiar with and, while doing so, to respond to our reading in a journal. We selected *The Goats* by Brock Cole, a book that we hoped might involve us intellectually as well as emotionally. For our journal responses, we decided to use the guidelines often given to students who are beginning this process. "Read a chapter and then stop to write a response to what you have read, using lead-in sentences such as "I wonder," "I think," "I didn't like...," etc. Given our busy schedules, we planned to read the book on our own and then to meet a month later for discussion. Both the individual work and the following group discussion gave us valuable insights about reading and writing processes.

While writing in my response journal, I found that the guideline to "stop to write after every chapter" created an artificial situation. Often I wished to respond as I read. At other times, I was dying to continue reading and strongly resented the need to stop. I was also aware that this same feeling *is* what makes some type of guideline important. Without it I would have slipped into the book, lost in the story and words, and written nothing after the third chapter.

Dealing with the "spell" of the story by stopping to write about our reactions points out one of the functions writing may play in Readers' Workshops. As I recorded my ideas, I was temporarily released from the enchantment of the text. I was able to examine the responses — both emotional and intellectual — that the book produced. Through this examination I gained a new awareness — of myself, of the reading-writing process and of the meaning of literature appreciation.

After a month, we held our "grand conversation," to use a term Maryann Eeds and Deborah Wells introduced us to. In order to focus after a hectic day of teaching, we went back to our response journals. Because we normally met as a literary study group, we began by examining our responses for any discussion of literary elements. Much to our surprise, our writing in our journals included much about these aspects of the book — without one "guiding" question from a teacher or professor! After sharing a couple of our responses, we just started to talk and continued to do so in an animated fashion for almost an hour.

Through the process we experienced the same excitement and learning that students in a workshop setting do as they talk about new books they are reading. We were able to check our perceptions of many of the book's events. We became aware of how differently others could experience the same words. And we often reconstructed our own understandings of the book because of the differing insights we gained from the conversation that afternoon.

Our experience put us in touch with our own reading behaviours and meaning-making, in touch with the power of others' thinking, and in touch with an easy way to convince others of the endless possibilities to Readers' Workshops. In reflecting on the process our group experienced, we realized how valuable such an experience could be to other teachers' moving in the direction of Readers' Workshops. Through their reading and their writing and their discussion, they too would be able to experience the reading-writing connection from the "inside out" (Atwell 1984).

In *On Being Literate* Margaret Meek has written, "Where a number of people read the same book, discussions promote different kinds of reflection, the taking on of another's viewpoint.... It is easier to explore learning from the written word in a group than in solitude" (p. 168). From the seemingly simple exercise of reading an unfamiliar book, pausing to write about it along the way, and then just talking about it together we had been "inside" that group experience we seek for our students. As teachers we need to remain aware of the processes involved in reading and we found that this experience of responding to our reading in writing and then discussing our insights with others was an excellent way of reminding us that reading is an ongoing process, that as we read and share our responses to that reading we are constantly gaining new insights, just as we hope our students will do.

We have continued to hold such study groups and have used our experiences in these groups as a footing for our work with fellow teachers who want to try Readers' Workshops for the first time or who want to understand firsthand the processes of reading as experienced in Readers'

Workshops. Teachers who themselves undergo the process of Readers' Workshops, will, like us, be able to answer their students' questions about responding in a journal from their own experience. They will also know for themselves the wonderful excitement of sitting at a table with a book and with people with whom to share and talk about that book.

References

Atwell, Nancie. 1984. "Writing and Reading Literature from the Inside Out." *Language Arts*. 61, 240–252.

Cole, Brock. 1987. *The Goats*. New York, NY: Farrar, Straus & Giroux Inc.

Eeds, Maryann & Deborah Wells. 1989. "Grand Conversations: An Exploration of Meaning Construction in Literature Study Groups." *Research in the Teaching of English*. 23, 4–28.

Meek, Margaret. 1991. *On Being Literate*. London, Eng.: The Bodley Head.

Workshops for Success

Three Teachers, Three Years, Three Workshops: A Story of Growing and Learning

Naomi Dahl, Angie Craigie and Myrna Reeves worked together during the years when they developed and grew along with their "communities of readers." **Naomi Dahl** *was the school's vice-principal and taught grades four, five and six over the three years. She has worked extensively with teachers and administrators in the areas of language learning and writing process.* **Angie Craigie** *had grade six students at the time and brings eleven years of teaching experience in upper elementary grades to this story of transition and change. She enjoys the excitement and enthusiasm students exhibit when they are involved in a community of readers.* **Myrna Reeves** *worked with the others as the school's teacher-librarian in a cooperative planning and resource capacity.*

Like most teachers and teacher-librarians, our objectives as educators are to encourage lifelong learning practices, to get our students hooked on books, and to develop the understanding in our students that literacy has great implications for them and for their futures. Our students should become more than simply adequate in literacy—they should achieve excellence.

Readers' Workshop, a concept first proposed to us by Blanche Lamont (see pages 24–43), provided an exciting vehicle for our students to achieve more than adequacy. Within its framework, our students achieved excellence. The essential ingredients of the workshop—choice, responsibility for learning, meaningful reading and writing experiences, decision making and talk—all served to develop ownership for learning in each student.

Our Readers' Workshop evolved over a three-year period with the same students. We began our search for excellence through the workshop format when Naomi's students were in grade four. Naomi and Myrna decided to start with a whole-class novel study. This decision arose in part from our need to include more literature in our theme-based reading program.

So, we all read *Jacob Two-Two Meets the Hooded Fang* by Mordecai Richler. Each student had a copy of the book and we read together chapter by chapter. Along with our reading, we introduced the idea of a response journal in which the students were to respond to what they were reading through writing and drawing. We discouraged the students from writing simple summaries of the chapters they had read. To support them in making their entries, we gave them a list of possible "thinking" lead-ins such as:

- I wonder what would happen if…
- It seems to me that…
- I liked the idea that…
- I predict…
- I question…
- I don't understand…
- This part reminds me of…
- etc.

We read aloud chapter one; then with the class as a whole we generated a group response to the chapter. We posted the class response to serve as a model for future responses. Then we continued to read, and both students and teachers responded to the reading in their journals.

The use of a response journal or a "thinking log" was a radical idea for our grade fours, but with teacher modelling, they gradually got "the hang" of it. Polished writing was not required, and spelling and punctuation were not formally evaluated. Rather, the journals were to be logs of response and understanding. We, in turn, commented in each of the student's journals to each of their responses with comments such as "Good point," "Very important," "I never thought of this before," etc. Our purpose was to focus the students' attention on the text and to assist them in unravelling the problems and progress of the story. In this supportive atmosphere, the students began to take more risks in responding in their journals, trying out their own predictions, disagreeing with others' opinions, or commenting on the characters' actions.

Our novel study ended satisfactorily, but not without a few inherent problems. We recognized that by using one novel, we had limited the children's choice, decision-making opportunities, talking and ownership in their learning.

The Workshop Evolves

As a result, when Naomi and Myrna implemented Readers' Workshop with the same students in grade five, we changed the rules in our community. We had a lot of work to do before we could begin our second Readers' Workshop. We realized we needed a bibliography of books — a whole selection of books from which the students could choose. Myrna's support as teacher-librarian was needed even more than before. Since we planned to have students work in small groups this time, we needed multiple copies of each title.

We scoured the library for hardcovers and paperbacks. Sets of novels used for whole-class study with grade five students previously were raided for our Readers' Workshop collection. Classroom libraries were ransacked. Some teachers ordered multiple copies of recommended titles through book clubs, and donated them to the library. An initial bibliography was keyed into the library computer. We attempted to cover as many areas of student interest as possible and to provide for various levels of reading ability. When we discovered gaps in our selection, we called on the resources of other school libraries. Paperbacks were purchased locally. We thought that a collection consisting of a minimum of two or three titles per student would be a good beginning. This collection would have multiple copies (two, three, four or more copies) of the same title. A final bibliography indicating author, title and number of copies available was produced for each student. Use of the computer simplified the generation of new bibliographies as titles were added or deleted. And, because by now other teachers in the school were beginning Readers' Workshops, the computerization helped them as well.

After the books were collected, borrower's cards were made for all materials that had been borrowed from other library collections. All the books were then displayed in a special Readers' Workshop section of the library. Only students participating in the workshop program at the time could sign out these books. After considering various methods, we found it most efficient to have students sign out the books as they usually did. We attached a removable coloured sticker to the book's pocket. This would alert us to return these titles to the Readers' Workshop section of the library. (In the future, when our collection has expanded significantly, we would like to integrate these materials back into the regular library collection so other students would have access to them. Having the books in the regular library collection would also cut down on the clerical work involved in managing these resources.)

While the large grouping of students with which we had worked in grade four had proved satisfactory, it was not as successful an experience as we had hoped. This grouping did not provide enough time for the students to talk about their books, nor did it meet their different interest needs. Consequently, with the grade fives, we formed groups of three to five students, with the students within each group working on the same novel. These groups were chosen by the students themselves with some guidance from us. We encouraged the students to pick people with similar interests and reading levels. Because friendship usually determined a groups' make-up, sometimes reading abilities varied widely. This wasn't always easily resolved and we still struggle with it.

Before the students divided into groups, we arranged for each of four staff members to present a book talk on a favourite title from the collection of books available to the students. We knew that a stimulating book talk included interesting anecdotes about the author. The library's reference books, picture collections and encyclopedias helped us to discover little known facts concerning the authors whose books had touched us. Our presentation of our favourite books and our anecdotes about the authors of those books served both to pique the interest of the children and to model our love of books. The power of this incentive should not be overlooked; students were fascinated by our choices.

The opportunity to choose their own groups worked well despite minor "first-time" disagreements which we helped resolve. Once the children formed their groups, they went off to the library to choose their books. They read out loud, they read to themselves, they read at recess and they read at home. Within their groups, they began to negotiate with one another about when and how much they should read outside of class. The groupings and the shared reading experiences worked like a charm!

Each day for the six weeks of our reading program, we allocated one hour to Readers' Workshop. The students knew that we expected them to read, to respond in their journals, and to talk about their reading. We structured their talk by giving the groups questions on cards. These questions dealt with the traditional concepts of characters, plot, mood, setting, etc. As time went on, the children would greet us with groans as they saw us approach with the "talk" cards. We persisted as we, the teachers, were not yet ready to give up control of the structure of the hour. When the children had completed each novel, they created visual displays to illustrate their books, choosing from dioramas, posters, book jackets, soap carvings, and the like. They then exhibited these in the library. The children read more than they ever had before and were very disappointed when the six weeks ended. Already they were looking forward to next year.

Growing into the Third Workshop

In the beginning of the third consecutive year for Readers' Workshop in our school, Angie joined us as we met to analyze the components of our program. Foremost in our minds was the fact that we needed to foster more student choice, more decision-making opportunities for the students, more reading and writing that was meaningful to the students and more opportunities for the students to talk about what they were reading. We had to give control to the students; we had to let them own what they were doing. In light of the fact that the students had two years' experience with the program and that they were grade six students, it was about time!! So we changed the format further.

This time, we enlisted the students' help in formulating our bibliography. Students were proud to share in making decisions that concerned them and they requested certain books. We teachers also added books from our list of reading material. In grade five, only teachers had presented their favourite books through book talks. This time all of the students in two grade six classes, Angie's and Naomi's, had the opportunity to share a favourite book with classmates during the workshop.

In class discussion, we and the students set goals for the number of books to be read in a certain period of time. Not only did we want to meet the needs of the students; we wanted to challenge them. We agreed on six books in a six-week period. This goal was open to negotiation between individual students and teachers.

The response journal remained an integral part of the program. The children's responses had become more sophisticated; they were very much at ease with this method of responding to literature. This time we asked that any illustrating in their journals be undertaken outside of the hour of class time in order that more time be spent reading, talking and writing.

Another major change was in the structure of the talk. We gave up our "talk cards." The children were talking about their books on their way to school, at recess, over lunch, during math, any time they could. With the students' permission, we taped some of their conversations during class and found their talk to be far more meaningful than anything that "talk cards" had produced. So we learned along with our students. We learned to trust their judgement and to have confidence in them.

The final change we made to our program was to include the students in the evaluation process. At the conclusion of Readers' Workshop, students completed a self-evaluation questionnaire. Students responded to questions about their reading skills, evaluated books and authors, and commented on the way the Readers' Workshop had been organized and run.

The first question, "What do you do to understand what you're reading?", brought a variety of responses. Many students made comments indicating that they used strategies while reading silently, such as "read to the end of the sentence; read slowly and reread the paragraph." Since students were organized into groups for the workshop, several included strategies such as "write in my journal and discuss with my group."

Students were asked to decide on favourite books and authors and to give reasons for their choices. As we know, grade six students love humour, suspense, adventure and action and these responses were included in many evaluations. The students commented that the author's knowledge about a topic is important. They enjoyed books written by authors "who understand kids."

During Readers' Workshop, students came to realize that it is okay to express negative opinions about books or parts of books. The most common reasons for disliking a book was lack of action. Students also decided some books were too difficult and some topics were not of interest. This latter view was expressed by one boy's comment about *Are You There, God? It's Me, Margaret* — "It talked about girl stuff!"

One question polled students for what they liked about and what improvements they would suggest in the organization of the workshop. Student choice in book selection was mentioned on almost all evaluations as being important to the success of the program. The fact that groups were self-directed for goal setting and for discussion of the books was also appreciated. Several students commented that they liked having a required minimum of books that they had to read since having such a goal made them work harder. They also enjoyed the variety of books and the accompanying book talks.

The areas where the students suggested improvements could be made included the need for a larger selection of books and for extra copies to accommodate communities of four to five students. Many also requested that Readers' Workshop run longer than the six weeks we allowed.

The question "How has Readers' Workshop affected you as a reader?" elicited many positive and exciting responses! The students really did come to view themselves as readers and felt that the expectations and intensity of the program had improved their reading skills. Comments included:

> "It got me reading more at home and at school." "It got me interested in books I never thought I'd read." "I can read better now." "I can read faster." "I like reading better now." "I found an author I really like." "It helped me understand books better." "I got to tell how I felt about books in my journal." "It improved my writing skills." [Children see the connection!] "I learned how to cooperate in a group and discuss books." "It has made me more alert and taught me how to express how I feel about a book."

Perhaps Jason's comment best sums up his classmates' enthusiasm for Readers' Workshop:

> "Before we started Community of Readers I didn't like reading and now I love it."

Readers' Workshop is not a new idea but, as we discovered for ourselves, its power is incredible. It involves students in meaningful reading and writing experiences. It gives them the opportunity to use language for genuine purposes. It fosters positive attitudes toward literacy. It empowers students through giving them opportunities to make choices and decisions according to their own needs and interests. Students become responsible for their own learning and progress.

The same sense of empowerment occurred for us as teachers. Our story shows how we evolved our practices over the three years. By the following year we were all three in different jobs, but we were profoundly changed by the collegial experience of planning and teaching together—and of learning together.

References

Blume, Judy. 1970. *Are You There, God? It's Me, Margaret.* New York, NY: Dell Publishing Co.

Richler, Mordecai. 1975. *Jacob Two-Two Meets the Hooded Fang.* New York, NY: Bantam Books.

Travelling in Time
with Readers' Workshop

*As a teacher-librarian **Linda F. Steen** has worked with language arts teachers to develop their classroom programs. In her fifteen years of experience she has also been a junior high school teacher of English, a consultant in gifted education, and a coordinator of enrichment programs for gifted students. Ms. Steen is concerned that teachers learn more about the books that will help involve students in reading. **Judy Osinski** has been an elementary classroom teacher for grades three through six in Edmonton and Calgary. During a recent placement with a grade six class Ms. Osinski found herself working with Ms. Steen, the school's teacher-librarian — and they both made changes to their teaching practices.*

Teachers are well-known scavengers, bargain hunters and collectors. Who else would buy not one, but twenty-four discarded copies of Janet Lunn's *The Root Cellar* for twenty-five cents each? After all, we might someday teach the right age group to enjoy this wonderful book about a girl who enters a root cellar and travels back in time to the days of the American Civil War. As it turned out, this bargain purchase at the public library sale led us to embark on a new experience with children's literature — the use of the Readers' Workshop format with a particular theme or genre of literature.

We had both just read Nancie Atwell's *In the Middle*, and from this reading we thought that the Readers' Workshop approach she described would help us achieve our objective of encouraging our students to become lifelong readers. We wanted to help our students to become "real readers" and agreed with Atwell that we could best do this by giving them personal choice in what they read, giving them time to read, and having them respond to their reading through writing and group discussion. It was our hope that by working together in groups, with the members of each group reading the same book, students would engage in genuine literary conversation. We hoped to hear them talk about character development and what the author was trying to say. We also hoped to hear them comparing the book to others they had read, giving their opinions about the writing and relating their own experiences.

Because we already had twenty-four copies of *The Root Cellar* and because it was an excellent book for grade six students—Judy was going to teach grade six in the following September—we decided on the theme of time travel for our first Readers' Workshop. Our excitement began to build at the prospect of implementing our first workshop at the beginning of the next school year. Everything was falling into place—except for the fact that there were going to be thirty, not twenty-four, students in the class! How might six more copies of *The Root Cellar* be acquired? Over a lunch hour when we were supposed to be paying attention to a staff meeting, we began to explore the idea of involving the students in the whole genre of time-travel fantasies, rather than borrowing six more copies of *The Root Cellar*.

As Michelle Landsberg stated, "…time-slip fantasies, in which the heroes slip backward and forward in time, are among the most enthralling of all children's books." We believed that our students would find time travel to be a highly motivating type of reading that would spark some lively discussion. After all, these students had a great deal of knowledge about time travel from their movie-going experiences and had been talking about the sequels of the film *Back to the Future*.

We searched the school library and asked other teachers to recommend any time-travel titles they knew of that were appropriate for grade six students. We also consulted children's literature references such as *Children's Literature in the Elementary School* by Huck, Helper and Hickman and *Michelle Landsberg's Guide to Children's Books* for annotated descriptions of quality literature related to our theme. Our research revealed a wealth of excellent literature, including *The Root Cellar*, that fell into the realm of time travel.

Having decided to "go for it," we loaded ourselves down with time-travel books and read furiously. We knew we were selecting books for a fairly typical grade six class that included a wide range of reading abilities and that would include two English-as-a-Second-Language (ESL) students. We narrowed our list to seven novels. Our choices varied from the less difficult *Time Cat* by Lloyd Alexander and *Mr. Z. and the Time Clock* by Bonnie Pryor to the more challenging *Playing Beatie Bow* by Ruth Park and *A Traveller in Time* by Allison Uttley. In addition to *The Root Cellar* by Lunn, we were pleased to find two other titles by Canadian authors, *The Doll* by Cora Taylor and *A Handful of Time* by Kit Pearson.

Now, we were getting closer to beginning a Readers' Workshop with the students. But first we needed to set procedures for them to follow. We recognized that even though we wanted their talk about the books to be authentic, open-ended, and fairly informal, with thirty students in the class the reading and discussing would need to take place in some sort of organized structure. We decided to begin each session with group discussions and to end with individuals reading and then responding in written form.

 # Getting into Readers' Workshop

To introduce the workshop format and the time-travel genre, Judy read aloud an eighth time-travel novel, *Tom's Midnight Garden*, to the students. She modelled the workshop process by having the students set a reading goal (how far Judy would read at a given reading), respond in their journals, and participate in small group discussions. The students were familiar with writing in response journals through a previous novel study. For this workshop, we asked them to write a question related to their reading at the conclusion of each journal response. We hoped that having to develop such questions would help initiate discussion within the groups. We posted a chart in the classroom to remind students of their responsibilities in both group and individual activities.

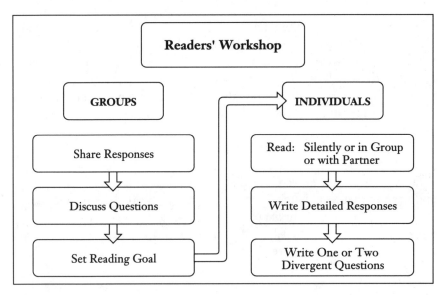

While students were learning the process, we discovered that their written questions did not always spark quality discussions of the teacher-read novel. At this point we gave a lesson on questioning strategies, introducing the concepts of convergent and divergent questions.

In this lesson, small groups were each given a picture and were asked to write as many questions as they could about their picture in five minutes. As the groups shared their questions we recorded them on the chalkboard under one of two headings: C or D. The students did not know that C stood for convergent and D meant divergent. Panic started to set in when we noticed the obvious absence of any divergent questions, so we modelled some. For example, since some of the pictures showed other places people lived, we asked, "Why do you think you might like to visit this place?" and "In what ways is this place different from Calgary?" Through our modelling we managed to get enough questions from the students to fill the D column.

By this point, the students were dying to know the meaning of C and D. Before revealing the terms, we had some fun with them by asking them to guess! They did notice a difference between the two types of questions, and a discussion ensued as to the usefulness of each type of question. The students recognized that convergent questions could be answered with one or two words, while divergent questions were open-ended and allowed for a range of possible answers. They agreed that divergent questions would be more appropriate for initiating discussions, and, therefore, would be the type to use in their response journals.

At last, we were ready to begin the workshop. We had obtained multiple copies of the chosen titles through inter-library loans. Then, we introduced the books to the students through book talks and allowed the students time for browsing. We asked the students what book they would like to read and with whom they would like to read, and then we formed groups of two to five members and assigned titles.

The members of each group decided together on the pace of reading they would follow and used their response journals as a basis for discussion of their novels. Students were not discouraged from reading ahead of their group, providing that they wrote responses in their journals as they read so they could share their responses in group discussions when all members of the group had reached the same point in the book.

Only a few groups had problems with their group members not keeping up with their reading; the students handled the problem themselves. For instance, Marcy and James sent homework to Sheryl, keeping her informed about the group's program when she was ill with a cold. Ken and Joel exerted pressure on Mark to do extra work at home when he fell behind in his reading.

After a few sessions, each student completed an evaluation form about the members of his or her group, rating them with regard to their work habits, group participation, discussion skills and quality of their questions. (Our students were accustomed to such peer evaluation from activities in Health and Social Studies classes.) These evaluation forms and subsequent discussions were useful in helping some students to set goals for themselves that would contribute to better group relations.

Reflecting on Readers' Workshop

As facilitators of the Readers' Workshop process, we were often amazed at the depth of insight that some of the students displayed in their responses. As Brian was nearing the end of *Mr. Z. and the Time Clock*, he began to question whether it was right to meddle with historical events while travelling in time. Kate commented on the improvement in a mother-daughter relationship that occurred in *A Handful of Time*. She noted that the daughter was more able to understand her mother's current problems after witnessing events of her mother's childhood. Trevor, who was reading *The Root Cellar*, wrote, "I think that Rose was really shy and unhappy when she first went to live with her Aunt Nan. But she became really confident because of the things that happened while she was in the past." Both Kate and Trevor were recognizing character development as important elements of their novels.

The discussion aspect of Readers' Workshop allowed students to support and assist one another. The two ESL students benefitted from oral reading and discussion of the chapters because their fellow group members provided background information to the plot and explained new vocabulary. In another group, students were presented with a good deal of strange dialect from nineteenth-century Australia while reading *Playing*

Beatie Bow. Neilu, Connie and Elaine found that oral reading of the novel sometimes helped to clarify the meaning of the unfamiliar language. They also spent time discussing the unusual words and phrases. Connie, who lacked confidence about her own reading ability, was particularly pleased when she was able to explain the meaning of the word "bairnie" which had stumped the others. Connie then began to view herself as someone who was quite capable of making contributions to the group.

Julie and Leslie, who chose to read the challenging novel *A Traveller in Time*, were mismatched in terms of their reading abilities. Although we had attempted to direct Leslie toward an easier novel, because we believed that she would be frustrated with her original choice, Leslie had insisted on reading *A Traveller in Time* with the promise that Julie was willing to help her with the reading. In the end, this is exactly what happened, with Julie acting as a reading mentor for Leslie. Both girls gained great satisfaction from completing the book.

As the Readers' Workshop progressed, we realized that the quality of the novel being read had a great bearing on the quality of discussion and written responses by students. The less difficult novels tended to be plot-oriented and focused less on character development. Written responses and oral discussions about these books were not particularly deep, even from the higher ability students. The more complex novels seemed to elicit a higher level of abstract thought, as students were able to discuss character development and relationships between people.

Grade six students have an involved series of grapevines through which important information is shared. We were pleased to see that the books they were reading rated highly enough to be discussed alongside "Do you think she likes me?" and the success of last night's volleyball game. Many students expressed an interest in reading more novels from our selection and the Readers' Workshop continued.

After the groups each read a second time-travel novel, we investigated specific aspects of the theme of time travel. We conducted a series of mini-lessons on time-travel devices, time periods visited, plausibility, character development, and time-travel themes. The students then compared the two novels they had read according to the topics we had introduced in the mini-lessons.

One of the highlights of our experience as teacher and teacher-librarian with Readers' Workshop was the opportunity to work as a team. We found it much easier to plan the processes involved in Readers' Workshop with two heads rather than one. We bounced ideas back and forth, set up objectives, made plans and team-taught lessons. We were also both able to join the community of readers in the classroom because we had read the same books as the students and could participate in discussions.

As a teacher-librarian, Linda gained some valuable experience that continues to assist her in cooperative planning sessions with other teachers who wish to use the Readers' Workshop approach. She became familiar with several new novels that she can recommend to students and has added some new time-travel novels to the library.

For her initial effort with Readers' Workshop, Judy found a theme approach very successful. She was able to read all the novels that the students were reading, which allowed for more meaningful teacher-student dialogue within the response journals and in discussions. Also, students really were motivated by the concept of time travel and were eager to read. Moreover, all members of the class shared a common bond in that they were all reading a time-travel book. Because the students were all reading novels in the same genre, inter-group discussions happened easily.

◇ Our Time Travel Continues

Long after our Readers' Workshop centred around time travel was concluded, the students continued to express interest in time-travel novels. We discovered other titles such as *Fog Magic* by Julia Sauer and *Earthfasts* by William Mayne, both of which had been gathering dust on our library shelves. These books were eagerly signed out by students and are still popular.

As teachers, our travel in time with Readers' Workshop continues in its own way. We are constantly learning new ways to use the workshop approach with our students. We take risks, try new things, experience successes and *un*successes since there are no failures — just opportunities for change and growth. Our colleagues have provided new ideas and support and our students have provided inspiration. The successes of this first Readers' Workshop experience gave Judy the confidence to branch out in her next Readers' Workshop by allowing her students to choose their group novels without consideration for the genre. Furthermore, they were free to choose from the library rather than from a teacher-chosen collection. Knowing that her students would, in fact, read and respond, and that they would be engaged thoughtfully in the process, Judy opened up the opportunities of choice. The theme was not as essential to the success of Readers' Workshop as was the shared process of reading.

And what about the twenty-four copies of *The Root Cellar*? Interestingly, the students had such a wide range of choices that we only required four copies of *The Root Cellar* at any given time. The urge to use the twenty-four copies as a class novel study has vanished and has been replaced by the desire to empower students to become real readers who exercise choice and take responsibility for their own learning.

FOR SALE

18 copies of *The Root Cellar* by Janet Lunn
available in convenient six-packs
25 cents each or $1.50 per six-pack
(Trades Welcomed)

 References

Time-travel Novels

Alexander, Lloyd. 1963. *Time Cat*. New York, NY: Dell Publishing Co.

Gareth, Jason's magical cat, takes the two of them on nine adventures into nine different historical eras. In each era, the relationship between humans and cats is explored.

Bond, Nancy. 1976. *A String in the Harp*. New York, NY: Penguin USA.

A Newbery Honor* book set in Wales, this story tells of a twelve-year-old American boy, Peter, who finds a harp key that once belonged to a great sixth-century Welsh bard. The key draws Peter back in time and takes him on a quest to return the key to its proper place.

Lunn, Janet. 1983. *The Root Cellar*. Toronto, ON: Penguin Books Canada Limited.

Sent to live with her aunt on Lake Ontario, Rose is terribly lonely until she enters a root cellar and travels back in time to Civil War days. There she makes friends with Will and Susan. When Will goes off to war, Rose and Susan make a difficult journey to try to find him.

Mayne, William. 1966. *Earthfasts*. London, Eng.: Hamish Hamilton.

The past comes to the present in the character of Nellie Jack John, an eighteenth-century drummer boy who marches right out of the earth in front of two village boys, David and Keith.

---

*The Newbery Honor awards are given annually by the American Library Association for contributions to American literature for children.

Park, Ruth. 1980. *Playing Beatie Bow*. London, Eng.: Puffin Books.

An Australian award-winning novel in which fourteen-year-old Abigail goes back to the nineteenth century where she is trapped for a year until she fulfills a prophecy and saves the Bow family. The author paints a very realistic picture of 1873 Sydney.

Pearce, Phillipa. 1958. *Tom's Midnight Garden*. London, Eng.: Oxford University Press.

A Carnegie Medal* winning novel about a boy who discovers a magical garden that he can visit at midnight. There he plays with Hatty, a child of the past. Eventually Tom discovers that Hatty is the same person as Mrs. Bartholomew, a little old lady who lives upstairs and has been dreaming of her past.

Pearson, Kit. 1987. *A Handful of Time*. Toronto, ON: Penguin Books Canada Limited.

While spending the summer at her cousin's cottage, Patricia finds an old watch that transports her back in time to the summer when her own mother was twelve.

Peck, Richard. 1989. *Voices After Midnight*. New York, NY: Delacorte Press.

Chad and his brother Luke hear mysterious voices late at night. As they explore their New York townhouse searching for the origins of the voices, they begin to slip in and out of their own time, back to the winter of 1888.

Pryor, Bonnie. 1986. *Mr. Z. and the Time Clock*. Minneapolis, MN: Dillon Press, Inc.

When Jerimy fixes an old clock, he and his twin sister, Julie, discover that the clock is a time-travel machine. They have adventures both forward and backward in time, always encountering the mysterious Mr. Z.

Sauer, Julia L. 1943. *Fog Magic*. New York, NY: Viking Penguin.

Greta, a young Nova Scotia girl, loves the fog and discovers that she can travel back into the past to a fishing village called Blue Cove by walking into the mist. This a Newbery Honor book.

---

*The Carnegie Medal and the Newbery Honor awards are among the many awards available for children's books. The Carnegie Medal is presented annually by the Library Association of England to the outstanding children's book written by a British author and published in England.

Taylor, Cora. 1987. *The Doll*. Saskatoon, SK: Western Producer Prairie Books.

When Meg's grandmother gives her an old doll to comfort her while she is ill, Meg goes back in time to pioneer days. There she becomes Morag, member of a family heading across the Canadian prairies.

Uttley, Allison. 1964. *A Traveller in Time*. New York, NY: Viking Press.

This English story is set in Edwardian and Elizabethan times. While visiting relatives named Thatcher who live on a farm in Derbyshire, England, Penelope opens a door and finds herself a part of the Thatcher family of 1582. She slips back and forth between families and finds herself a participant in a plot to try to help Mary Stuart, Queen of Scots, escape from imprisonment by Elizabeth I.

Atwell, Nancie. 1987. *In the Middle: Writing, Reading, and Learning with Adolescents*. Portsmouth, NH: Boynton/Cook Publishers Inc.

Huck, Charlotte, Susan Hepler, and Janet Hickman. 1987. *Children's Literature in the Elementary School*. New York, NY: Holt, Rinehart and Winston Inc.

Landsberg, Michelle. 1986. *Michelle Landsberg's Guide to Children's Books*. Toronto, ON: Penguin Books Canada Limited.

Who's Doing the Learning Around Here?

Carla Watson has taught preschoolers, upper elementary grade students, and adults in continuing education courses, but now teaches at a grade two level. After returning to teaching at the elementary level from being home with her own two children, Ms. Watson states she did not feel like an expert but felt that she had a lot to learn from her students and peers, and from courses and educational sources. In this piece, she shares her process of learning.

In the fall of the first year that I decided to "risk" using Readers' Workshops with my grade two classes, I was using stories with my students that fit into various themes drawn from two literature-based reading series. At the same time, the students and I were sharing other theme-related pieces of literature from trade books. To prepare my grade twos for the procedures they would be using in Readers' Workshop, I began having them read the stories in partners, letting them make their own decisions on whether to take turns reading paragraph by paragraph or page by page. In whole-class mini-lessons, I did a lot of modelling, responding orally to the reading selections with the class as a group. I encouraged the students to respond orally to their partners as they read the selections, and then we shared their thoughts in the large group.

My next step was to encourage the students to put their responses down in written form. Once again, I modelled written responses. As well, I posted two charts with samples of sentence starters such as "I wonder…" and "I liked…" that the students could use as needed to help them get started in their writing. I encouraged them to give reasons for why they felt the way they did about what they had read.

I made overheads of many of the students' responses and the class examined them and made suggestions about the content as they were used to doing in Writers' Workshop.

While the students and I were laying the groundwork for Readers' Workshop, I went through the library and selected all the books of which we had multiple copies that were appropriate for grade two students. I went through them all for interest level and reading difficulty — and read as many of them as possible! I then set up an inviting reading centre for the students in one corner of the room.

When I thought that my second-graders, and I, were ready to read in small groups and to respond to books together within those groups, I prepared to ease them into this stage of greater independence by grouping them homogeneously — with others of similar reading abilities. Hoping to ensure their success, I matched these groups of two to five students with books I thought were appropriate. I also provided each student with his or her own response journal which the student was to keep in the reading centre.

To get the members of each group started, I sat in on a pre-reading conference with them while they discussed the title, cover, author, what they thought the book was going to be about, and so forth. The students then took turns reading their book orally, with everyone in the group following along. Some books had tapes and the students listened to the tapes as they read along a second time. Each group had a "status sheet" on which the members recorded the title of the book, the date and the page the group read to each day. The students invited me to a post-reading conference in which they would retell the story and we would discuss their predictions and questions. The students then wrote in their response journals. I later read their entries and replied to them. After the students had written their responses, I encouraged the groups to "extend" or celebrate their stories by choosing from a number of activities such as making posters, radio commercials, dramatic portrayals, report cards on the characters, and storyboards.

Unfortunately, things were not working out exactly as planned. Most of the books I had selected were fairly short and I found that I was becoming frustrated because I could not get around to every group before the group members had finished reading their books. The weaker readers didn't have group members to model discussing the books, or to bring up points beyond the "I liked..." variety, so they were quickly at a loss as to what they should be doing. They weren't drawing on our previous mini-lessons about responding and about working in groups.

After much thought, I decided that I had to change tactics. I decided to make the groups bigger and to create groups that were more heterogeneous. I reasoned that although the less able students would have more difficulty with some of the selections, they would gain from the modelling of and discussions with more able classmates. Moreover, students in heterogeneous groups bring different backgrounds to the discussions which helps to influence and broaden all of the students' perspectives.

Soon the students were constantly asking when it was time to read. The successes mirrored in the students' improved reading and continued enthusiasm towards the workshop approach gave me the determination to try Readers' Workshops again in the following school year.

Reflections and discussions with other teachers in Readers' Workshop interest groups (see pages 150–153) and with my school colleagues helped to give me the confidence to make more changes to the program and to re-evaluate my own role in the workshop. In the first year of the workshop, I had been so concerned about doing everything the "right" way that I had tended to take control of the conferences and discussions with the students. I now felt that it might be more beneficial to the students if I became more of a facilitator.

Thus, although I approached Readers' Workshop in the second year in some of the same ways as I had in the first, for example using group sessions and mini-lessons to introduce the students to the procedures they would use in Readers' Workshop, I made a number of changes.

I wanted the students to take more ownership for their groups and so I allowed the members of each group to work out how they would take turns speaking in discussions, reading, and even choosing books. One group decided to use the library's copy number on the outside of the books for the order of reading and speaking. Another group used a popsicle stick to be passed around to determine who had the floor. When there were difficulties with the group dynamics, I tried not to interfere but to let the group work it out. Sometimes I needed to intervene, as was the case when one group decided to do their reading by letting the members of the group take turns reading the selection "silently" — while the others waited for their turn!

Another area I tried to let go of was the choosing and assigning of the books to be read. I had over fifty sets of books in the room. During the first class I let the students explore all the books to find those that they felt comfortable with and were interested in reading. Initially I grouped the students myself to be sure there was a mix of abilities, and some strong participants in each group, but the students picked their group's books. Later as the students became more knowledgeable, it was the shared interest in a particular book that determined who was in a particular group! If there weren't enough copies of a given book, the students simply shared! Being allowed to choose the books themselves acted as a catalyst. The students could hardly wait to get started. We were off!

In my second year using the workshop approach, I also started introducing and teaching parents and guardians about Readers' Workshops through articles in our monthly class newsletter. I reasoned that if I had the parents' and guardians' understanding and support, both the students and I would gain. I also wanted to try and have at least one parent/guardian volunteer in the classroom each day for the hour of Readers' Workshop to help with the groups. I asked for volunteers and prepared a background sheet of information for them and "trained" them to work with the groups under my guidance. The volunteers had a sheet on which to write their observations. I felt that this record helped to give me a written record of the groups that I couldn't get to that day and, as well, the records helped to make the parents/guardians feel more involved by recording their contributions to the success of the program.

I was determined that the parent/guardian volunteers and I should try to act more as facilitators than as directors in the pre-reading and post-reading conferences. Yet I found that it was very difficult for me to let go

of control and I had to realize that doing so was my problem and not the students'.

As the volunteers and I circulated and listened in on the groups, I was amazed at the discussions that were taking place in some groups. I found that, at first, as soon as I arrived and tried to sit on the outside of their circle, the students would move over to include me and all the eye contact would shift from their peers to me. However, once they realized that I was there just to listen and to make the odd comment, they got on with the business at hand.

I was learning so much about how my students thought, their interpersonal skills and work habits, and the connections they were making between books and their own lives. One group of boys was discussing *Molly the Brave and Me* in a pre-reading conference. Jim, who comes from a single-parent family where the father is raising him and his brother, had peeked into the book and was predicting to the others in the group that the "I" in the story must be a boy because girls couldn't climb and balance on a jungle gym and girls didn't like bugs. The other group members didn't realize how Jim's background was influencing the connections he was making and a very heated discussion took place about girls and boys.

As in all groups, there were quiet members and those who wanted to dominate the discussions. As facilitators, we tried to remind groups that everyone needed a turn. Nevertheless, it was interesting to see how some students became adept at avoiding giving their opinions because the group would want to know why they thought what they thought about something.

At the beginning of the year when we had worked together as a class reading and discussing shared selections in preparation for Readers' Workshop, the students had been writing thoughtful responses. But when they began to write their individual responses to their reading done in small groups, I was really disappointed in their efforts. I was forced to ask myself why the responses were so much less thoughtful than when we had been together as a whole class.

It occurred to me that I had approached the various methods of celebrating the completion of books differently and in much more detail this year than I had in last year's workshop. Instead of just offering a wide variety of activities to extend or celebrate the stories, I carefully introduced the projects individually, modelling and discussing them in great depth. Hence the celebration had become more important than the responding. As I did some more modelling of how to respond to reading, the student responses began to improve. The students were keen to be the "mystery writer" whose response was displayed on the overhead.

Another factor that contributed to my own learning through my experiences with Readers' Workshop was the commitment I made to help other teachers who were just beginning to work on Readers' Workshops. Interested teachers in my own school and from other schools came to observe my grade two class working in Readers' Workshop. I think that the visits from other teachers helped influence many of my students to choose "chapter books" to read. They didn't want to be observed reading books with lots of pictures that they considered to be babyish or too easy, even though in many cases the minimal vocabulary in these books was actually quite difficult. I had numerous parents come to me to ask what had inspired their children to want to read the chapter books. This demand for chapter books created a problem because it is difficult to locate books of this type that are at the grade two reading and interest level and yet have some literary merit. One solution was to introduce more non-fiction books. These met with some success, but the need for more chapter books still remains an ongoing problem.

The learning that was taking place in Readers' Workshop spilled over into the students' writing, art and free reading. One group of students had really enjoyed reading *The Magic School Bus* books. When we were working on a space unit, two of the girls, Carrie and Nicole, decided to write their own book about the class going into outer space on the bus using a format similar to *The Magic School Bus* books.

Through their work in Readers' Workshops, my students have become more aware of setting and character development in stories and often comment on these elements when they share their pieces of writing in class. Yes, my students have definitely been learning this year. But I have found that I have personally assimilated so much more from the parents/guardians, other teachers, and most important, from my students. By relinquishing some control and allowing my students to take some responsibility and leadership in their groups, I have been learning much about my students, about myself, and about the way learning occurs. I must wonder, "Who is doing the learning around here?"

References

Cole, Joanna. 1986. *The Magic School Bus at the Waterworks*. New York, NY: Scholastic Inc.

O'Connor, Jane. 1990. *Molly the Brave and Me*. New York, NY: Random House Inc.

On Blooming: A Collaborative Exploration of Reading and Writing Process

Michelle Bastock has taught from kindergarten through grade eight in Saskatchewan and Alberta. Of her nine years' experience, five have been with grade one. She especially enjoys working with emergent readers and writers. Toni L. Marasco has taught all elementary school grades in her twenty-five years of experience, as well as having worked in remedial reading, as a school system language arts consultant, and in elementary school administration. Ms. Marasco was the principal of Ms. Bastock's school at the time Ms. Bastock began to change her approach to early reading instruction.

Today I walked into my grade one classroom and the room was quiet—well, as quiet as a grade one class can be. The children were reading books of their own choice. We are arriving...the children are blooming...they see themselves as readers and writers and they are involved with both.

How did they bloom? I wondered, as I mused over a quote from Robert Krauss' *Leo the Late Bloomer*: "A watched bloomer never blooms." I had realized as we set out on our journey at the beginning of the school year that we needed to create a place where it was safe to bloom and where risks could be taken freely—an environment where experimentation was welcomed and approximations applauded—and so from the outset the students and I worked hard together to create the necessary environment.

Things started to happen the day Shane brought in part of his coin collection to share with the rest of the class. The other children asked him questions, made comments and encouraged him to write about his coin collection in his writing book. He used all the strategies he knew to write; he was an expert and he wanted to share his knowledge with others. We published his book and he presented it at the "Author's Chair," where the class gathers daily to listen to student authors read pieces of their writing.

Shane's presentation encouraged others to share and write about their special interests. In the days that followed, Aileen brought and shared her sea shell collection. She then wrote and published. Cristal brought her pin collection.... The children enjoyed sharing their special interests and writing about them. By Halloween everyone had published at least one book.

The free choice of what to write about, combined with coaching of ideas and strategies, continuous nudging and mini-lessons, invited all the children to become writers. During "Author's Chair" discussions, children often asked the author, "Where did you get that idea?" The responses varied but, as the children were exposed to more literature, the answer was often, "I got the idea from a book." We talked about how writing helps reading and, how reading helps writing.

The Principal's Thoughts

What's happening? All of these bright, eager faces clutching wallpaper-bound books—tugging at sleeves—begging to share. They come alone, in pairs or in clumps—at recess, lunch and during free-choice reading time—anxious to read their newly published manuscripts. If I'm busy they'll hop on the secretary's knee; if not, they bound right in, their enthusiasm spilling over. Sometimes I have books stacked on the table and promise to take them home for "homework" and to write something special in "Notes to the Author." I am amazed at the confidence and skill of these young authors so early in the school year.

Just before Christmas we began our weekly free-choice reading cycle. Every Monday morning, I recorded each child's free-choice selections for that week. These were books the children would present to their partners in the grade five class at their shared reading sessions on Friday mornings. I checked the children's choices to be sure they were appropriate or "just right." It quickly became apparent that many of the children needed help to figure out which books were appropriate and we began to discuss what made a book "just right." "Just right" books, we decided, are books that will help them become better readers — books they are able to read. The rule of thumb was: If you have to skip over more than three words on one page it is probably a "challenge" book and a bit too hard for now.

If I found that some of the children's choices were inappropriate, we discussed alternative choices and I gave them other suggestions. Sometimes this process would result in the children choosing two or three selections for that week. The children practised reading their selections all week to prepare for reading with their grade five partners on Friday.

During the Friday sessions, the grade one and the grade five children took turns reading to one another. Then my grade one children recorded titles and authors of the books they had read to their grade five partners, as well as comments and/or illustrations about their reading, in their reading logs. When my students came together for sharing sessions they read to one another from their logs, sharing their comments about characters and their descriptions of favourite parts in the books they were reading. In sharing their reading logs they invited one another to read other books. As happens with literate persons they learned about new books from others and shared their own choices in return. In this way they all participated in the world of literature that they'd been reading.

After Christmas I noticed new additions to the children's book baskets. (The children are seated at tables and have plastic baskets of books at each table.) Before Christmas, most of the books in the basket had been easier predictable selections that I had chosen and that we had read together in small groups. All of a sudden, these baskets were overflowing with new books. I realized that the children were branching out and choosing other books from around the classroom. Their initiation of this new level of "ownership" for what was in the book baskets demonstrated to me their growing interest in reading. That was my cue — we needed more reading material. I obtained some money from our principal and bought some books for our class library.

Because it was only part way through the first school year I had to be selective. My students were not independent readers yet! I needed to find books for which the children had some background knowledge and that covered a variety of reading levels. The Ladybird books fit the bill. Most were well-known fairy tales revised to enable children to work towards independence in reading. I purchased about thirty of them at an appropriate range of reading levels for my particular class. The Monday morning I presented these books was an exciting one! The children were seen everywhere in the school with books under their arms looking for someone to read to. The impact of these books was evident in their writing soon afterward. Many children were creating their own versions of these fairy tales which in turn influenced the writing of other students. The link between literature and writing was solidifying.

We then began to link other literature-based activities to this cycle. For example, character puppets, interviews and riddles provided opportunities for extending reading and writing. As a result of these activities children began to look around for other books. Now on Mondays before free-choice selections were made, I presented new books — sometimes a number of books in the same genre, at other times author collections matched to the children's interests and abilities. I also presented authors. The day I presented Mercer Mayer the children insisted that I read all of his books to them that morning in one sitting!

The Principal's Thoughts

> Books! Books! Books! Ever in search of more reading material. The budget is spent — what now? I offer some of my personal library — some of my favourites and some that I know will appeal to my young friends. I look forward to "book talking" with the children and wonder which books from my own collection to select next. Cowboys — yes I know they like cowboys — Frank Asch, Norm Birdwell, yes I think...

In February, I attended the CEL (Child-centred Experience-based Learning) Conference in Winnipeg where Nancie Atwell presented the idea of students writing letters to one another in which they discussed books they had read or were reading. The next week I asked the grade fives to write response letters to the grade ones about the books they had shared. The letters included compliments on reading progress and questions about favourite authors and books. The grade one children were intrigued! Someone was writing to them about their books and their reading. They decided to write back — another link between reading and writing.

The development of the "Reader's Chair" evolved from the "Author's Chair." It provided a vehicle to share reading proficiency and literature awareness. Children prepared books to present in turn, but spontaneous presentations were accommodated as well. The child presenting (sometimes the children presented in pairs, if support was desired) might read the whole book, a favourite part, the beginning, middle or end. After the reading, the group would ask questions or offer comments. This was an opportune time to teach elements of literature in context. "Reader's Chair" became a popular activity—we never ran short of willing presenters.

Over the year the children have learned to:

- choose books at appropriate levels
- publish books based on their free-choice writing
- connect reading experiences to their writing
- become risk-takers
- understand the importance of preparation and rehearsal in order to share with an audience
- view themselves as readers and writers
- see their progress as they moved from reading "just right" books to reading "challenge books"
- enjoy and value reading and writing
- work with cross-graded buddies
- share opinions, dialogue and responses
- write letters as a form of communication
- extend ideas into fine arts
- respond freely to their own interests in books

One day in May, Cristal came to me and asked, "What is 26 plus 16 plus 21?" When I figured it out, her eyes lit up and she said, "Mrs. Bastock, I read sixty-three pages today. I read three books." The children really are blooming. Blooming in May is a wonderful part of grade one. Reading and writing for real purposes has made the process rewarding and exciting for both me and the children.

The Principal's Thoughts

How can the principal be involved in this marvellous process—become part of the unfolding of young minds? Very simply—get involved! The key is to be supportive and encouraging—to keep the door open and be readily available to students and teachers. Yes, even when you are busy! Visit classrooms often, stay if invited and help out. Publishing is a very labour-intensive job. Sharing requires someone to share with and the wealth of experiences children share provides you with a special dimension and understanding of each child's unique situation. Teachers need opportunities to share as well—to celebrate successes, to ponder new routes and to get a boost when they're exhausted with the pace. Provide resources—books, publishing materials, furniture, support personnel, volunteers and most of all, your time. Yes, children bloom, but such blooming takes that special nurturing, that ray of sunshine, that sprinkle of moisture and that burst of nutrients that only a committed teacher can give.

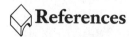

References

Krauss, Robert. 1971. *Leo the Late Bloomer.* New York, NY: Windmill Books, Inc.

Reading for Success: Readers' Workshop in the Early Grades

*These three authors exemplify the sharing and interaction that has characterized the growth of Readers' Workshops in Calgary and its surrounding districts. **Debra Morgan** has taught throughout the elementary grades for seven years. She writes of her experience with Readers' Workshops for year two students and at present teaches in a multi-aged classroom with students in their second and third years of school. **Peggy Murakami** has been developing her Readers' Workshop approaches over the past three years with grade one students in a low socio-economic area. Ms. Murakami's teaching experience is from kindergarten level through grade two. She has team-taught with Diane Perry and worked with her teaching colleagues to develop Readers' Workshops at Terrace Road Elementary. **Diane Perry** currently teaches in a multi-aged classroom with students in their second and third years of school. Her use of Readers' Workshops has also been with first-year students who were from needy home settings. Ms. Perry has specialized in early childhood teaching from kindergarten through grade four in Alberta schools. All three teachers draw upon their multiple experiences to show that Readers' Workshops are successful for their children no matter what the children's backgrounds.*

All three of us believe strongly that Readers' Workshops best meet the needs of our students and our needs as individual teachers. The grade one children Peggy is currently working with have had relatively little exposure to books before entering school, while the grade two children Debra and Diane are working with were very familiar with books when they started school. All these children experience success in our Readers' Workshops; even our nonreaders become excited about books and reading.

Our main goal is to guide the children towards becoming actively involved in the reading process. Central to this purpose is the aspect of choice. Our belief—a belief reinforced by our experiences with Readers' Workshops—is that giving children choice about their reading material stimulates their interest and develops motivation to read. To make this principle of choice work effectively means providing the children with an opportunity to choose from a wide variety of literature written specifically for children. We then guide and monitor the children's selection process to ensure they choose books that they will be able to read alone and in groups.

We expose the children to a wide variety of genres — poetry, fairy tales, adventure, mystery, biography, etc. Both fiction and nonfiction books are made available. A rule of thumb we use when we are choosing books for our children is that the books we've found interesting, the children will like as well. Readers with controlled vocabulary are often boring for adults and are just as likely to be boring for children as well. As adult readers we expose ourselves to a wide variety of choices, and then choose what we feel drawn to out of our own life experiences and interests. This same principle is true for children. Seven-year-old Neil's comment illustrates the rightness of his choice for him: "I like this book. In a way I think that this book makes me feel like I'm in it. That's what I like in a book—when I feel I'm in a book."

In order to help the children to become aware of their choices, we do a lot of book talks. We sit on the floor with the children and a stack of books. We talk about why we like a particular book. We look at the pictures and have the children comment on them.

Predicting is a crucial part of the reading process and one we often model during book talks, as well as at other times. We encourage the children to make predictions and to test their hypotheses as they read or listen. One approach to predicting is to read the inside flap of a book jacket or back cover and make predictions about the book in light of the information found there. Sometimes we might read a few lines or pages from a book and again have the children make predictions based on this reading. If we are looking at a book that is divided into chapters, we often read the title of a chapter and have the children predict what the chapter might be about.

These book talks are an ongoing form of instruction where we examine different parts of a book. Aspects of books that we look at and discuss with the children are the spines of books, the inside flaps of book jackets, the back covers, authors, dedications, chapter titles, the index and anything else that we think is relevant. We talk at length about authors so that the children realize that authors are just regular people like them. This understanding then carries over into the children's writing and they begin to see themselves as authors who write for themselves and for an audience. We have children in our classes who have announced with pride and confidence that they are going to be authors when they grow up.

Children need lots of time to read in a positive, risk-free environment. Providing this environment and the time for reading is central to Readers' Workshops. Children learn to read by reading: often, children need to see a word forty times before it becomes part of their reading vocabulary. In Peggy's classroom, parent/guardian volunteers come in and share books with the children. The goal is for each child to have a one-to-one reading experience with an adult at least once a week. All our children also have a reading buddy from another grade. Our classes and their buddy classes read together on a regular basis. Other schools have successfully initiated "grandparent" programs, where senior citizens come into the school on certain days and read individually with children. By arranging for our children to read with other people, of all ages, we give them other "audiences." They have a reason to prepare to read well aloud and, by reading with someone else, one more opportunity to gain the fluency that comes from re-reading familiar material. Furthermore, they are able to hear the different perspectives and reactions to their books or stories. They join a larger community of readers.

Reading can take many forms. We read aloud at least once a day to our children, and more to children who haven't been read to very much at home. Even our children who are fluent readers enjoy being read to. We also have the children do a variety of oral and silent reading individually, with partners, and in groups. The methods we choose depend on what our focus is at a particular time.

With grade ones we do a lot of teacher reading, and oral partner reading. Grade one children are very egocentric and we've found that they love an audience — even when the audience is not listening! When children first begin to read with one another, they will often read their individual books aloud at the same time quite happily.

Many children enter grade one believing they will learn to read the first day; we want to help the children maintain this positive attitude. We constantly reinforce the children's ability to read and we talk about them as

readers. When children say they can't read, we model how to read pictures. Throughout the school year we continue to talk about reading in terms of reading pictures. We start beginning readers with patterned and repetitive books, and also do a lot of chanting using charts. Listening centres are another valuable way to help children associate print with spoken text, and to further enhance their background of experience with literature. At the centre with a taped version of a book, the children are able to be "read to" as often as they wish.

We still read aloud to our grade two children every day, but they also do a lot of shared and partner reading. Each group cooperatively chooses the book they want to read, from either the classroom or the school library. Our goal is to have the children share the experience of reading with one another, and to develop a community of readers who read and share their responses to the books they read with one another and with the teacher.

We believe that children learn what they observe. Thus teacher modelling is crucial to our Readers' Workshops and must be ongoing — modelling the same things over and over again in a variety of ways. Once is not enough for learning to occur.

Watching the children grow as readers is very exciting. They quickly pick up the language we model for talking about books. It is fascinating to listen to them talk to their classmates about the books they are reading. They love to recommend books they have enjoyed to others.

We encourage the children to respond both orally and in writing to the literature they read. Too often it is easy for us as adults to assume that children think as we do, and that concepts such as responding to books don't need to be taught. However such concepts do need to be taught and re-taught. For instance, we have encountered children who are unaware that creating meaning is the goal of reading. This understanding then needs to be taught; children need to understand *why* they are reading.

We teach the children how to discuss the books they read through oral discussions which we call conferences. Through these conferences we want to help the children to develop and expand their thinking. We model conferencing continuously in large group settings, with small groups, and with individuals. We want to support the children in getting to the stage where they become independent in conferencing and are able to conference with one another without our involvement. Ideally, we like to have groups of two or three students who read and conference together. However, this size of group is not a realistic goal for all grade ones since children need a certain degree of maturity before they can handle conferencing with other children. Our grade two children are becoming skilled at conferencing with one another.

Conferencing can occur at any stage in the reading process. Predicting is a form of conferencing, stopping part way through a book to discuss it is conferencing, and discussing written responses is also conferencing. The processes we use during conferences show our children how to comprehend and to confirm or to evaluate predictions made about the story. Areas that we address during conferences include story elements such as plots, setting, and characterization. Other discussions centre around how the author gains and sustains the reader's attention, and how the story relates to experiences the children have had.

We also want the children to respond in writing to the literature they read. They record their written responses in reading or response logs, which can be in a variety of formats such as teacher-made booklets, fully lined scribblers or notebooks with half-blank and half-lined pages.

With grade one children oral responses are the first step towards written responses. We start with group oral responses; after the children have had time to read their books we have four or five of them share their favourite pictures and parts of the book with the whole class.

Another step towards written responses that we use is pictorial responses where the children are asked to draw pictures of their favourite parts of a book or story they have read. Children's art is a very special expression of their individuality. As the children's skills develop they will progress from picture responses to combination picture and written responses, and then to written responses. Mark, a grade one student, drew a scene from his book and then wrote, "I like the part when Rosie went for a walk. It was funny when the fox fell in the hay."

From the beginning we write replies to the children's responses. We have the children begin their responses with "Dear Mrs. Perry" (teacher's name), and we begin our reply to them with "Dear Erin" (their names). Using this letter format provides strong motivation for children to write about the books and stories they read because it sets up a written dialogue between the child and the teacher. We sometimes have the children share their written responses with the class—student modelling thus becomes another mode of teaching.

Responding in writing to every book read is not necessary and may in fact take the joy out of reading and turn it into a goal-directed task. Each of us develops our own criteria as to how often we expect the children to respond on paper. Peggy has her grade one children respond almost daily until they begin to read longer books. Debra and Diane use once a week as a guideline: this requirement seems like a lot to some children, while others want to respond more frequently.

We always encourage the children to write a variety of responses, such as "I like the part where...," I thought it was funny when...," "I wonder...," "I hope...," "I wish...," and "My favourite character is...." The children need lots of exposure to different kinds of response. We sometimes stop part way through reading a story to the children and model the "I wonder..." or the "I predict..." response. After we read a story or a chapter we discuss it with the children, and encourage them to respond to various aspects of the story. For instance, we might ask them to complete the sentence "I thought it was funny when...," or "My favourite character is...because...". Another approach is to ask them what certain events in the story remind them of; this approach usually generates a lively discussion. Another way we model responses is in the way we frame our written replies to the children's responses in reading logs.

While we have used and continue to use response sentence starters with the children to help them get started with their responses, we are finding that these sentence starters are very similar to story starters. Just as story starters have been shown to limit the children's written output, so the sentence starters for response seem to outlive their usefulness. Part of our process of growth is thus to guide the children away from using the sentence starters. Peggy, after reading to her class, often asks the open question, "Does anyone have anything they want to say about this story?" She then encourages the children to write about their thoughts in their reading logs. Our goal is to encourage spontaneous and divergent responses in the children *not* just "answers" to questions or to prompts. Whatever pops into a child's head about the reading is often where he or she is ready to begin his or her response.

Some children typically write very short, unelaborated responses in their reading logs and quickly develop one pattern of responding, such as "I like the part…". As part of our teaching and evaluating, we continuously monitor the children's responses, and develop a sense of when a child is ready to move on in his or her individual process of growth. What we are looking for, and encouraging, is development in the way the children think about what they read. We want the children to establish a personal connection with what they read, and to develop their ability to reflect on what they have read. Diane and Debra usually write at least one question in their replies to entries in each of the children's logs and expect the children to answer it. With her grade ones, Peggy often asks a question orally about the child's response, and moves into written questions as she senses the child is ready. The children can also write questions to their teacher. Sara, a grade two student, wrote in her log, "Why do they talk about different people all the time a chapter changes?"

Teacher replies to student entries are crucial so we write back as soon as possible: our goal is to respond within twenty-four hours. While reading logs require a significant amount of teacher time and writing, they make it possible for us to bring more out of our children's responses, to amplify and extend both the children's experiences with books and their thinking.

Simultaneously, the reading logs let us evaluate students' abilities to go beyond superficial "I like…" responses, and then to relate their reading to their own experiences.

Reading logs can also be used in other contexts. We sometimes have our grade two children take their reading logs with them for conferences with their reading groups. They share their written responses with one another, and initially this helps to focus their discussion. Kristen, a grade two student, wrote in her log, "It's sad and happy." She then went on to describe her views about what was sad and happy in the book she was reading. Reading this passage from her log to her group could generate a discussion about what the other group members found sad and happy. In another part of her log, Kristen made reference to an event that she found scary. A discussion about why this event was scary might begin, and extend to the kinds of happenings that the children find scary in their lives.

We believe that there is a strong reading/writing connection: that children write what they read. If they read books with interesting words and varied sentence structure, their writing will echo that. If they read books with limited vocabulary and sentence structure, then their writing will reflect that. One of our students once started a sentence in her story with the word "often" — "Often dragon and monster would…". When her teacher commented on this new addition to her writing style, her response was that she had noticed that sentences in the books she had read sometimes started that way.

Readers' Workshops get children HOOKED on books and on reading. Children in Readers' Workshops grow to love books and read far more than children do in the more traditional reading programs we've experienced. Our children are book-literate and we believe that what we have done has helped to make them that way.

Readers' Workshop: Teach Me, If You Dare!

Susan West has shared her love for literature at various grade levels for ten years. She still enjoys the challenge as seen in this account of her experiences with grades six, seven, and eight students.

When I entered my junior high classroom in September, I had such hopes for the year to come. I had experimented with Readers' Workshops for three years at the elementary level, and I was dizzy with their success. Now, I wanted to share my love of literature with older students, certain they, too, would benefit from the program.

Readers' Workshops, Me, and My Elementary Students

My students at the elementary level had taught me that not everybody is interested in the same things. Indeed, one of the features they had particularly liked about Readers' Workshops was that they could choose the books they wanted to read. Jeffrey, in grade six, and a student of mine for two years, had said about Readers' Workshops:

> "You get to read a lot of good books. I like it better than when your teacher picks a book and everyone in the class has to read it….Like girls might not want to read adventure books where everybody's getting killed and it's gory. Boys might not want to read stuff about ponies."

Despite Jeffrey's male bias, I felt he had a point. In the workshop approach, students can select what they want to read from a wide variety of books. There is far less teacher direction in the workshop setting than there is in more traditional classrooms, although in Readers' Workshops teachers often still put together the initial selection of novels from which the readers may choose. Teachers in workshops also may provide "lead-ins" and questions that are designed to provoke the students' thoughts about their reading.

My elementary students had also enjoyed the shared learning aspect of Readers' Workshops. Jodie was an avid reader, and, like Jeffery, a student of mine for two years. She enjoyed working in a group:

"Working in a group gives me confidence, like when someone else says I have a good idea….You can have your own opinion, but the group work helps me develop my ideas. I like to have a bunch of different opinions."

I had had my elementary students meet in groups of two or three or four. The groups talked about the novels they were reading and shared their thoughts and experiences before writing anything down. It was exciting to hear the students use literary terms such as "setting," "conflict" and "imagery," and to listen to them try to persuade their peers to their opinions. The students and I set some "ground rules" at the beginning to make the discussions more productive and to prevent arguments. For example, each group was led by a chairperson, a position that rotated to each member of the group. It was the chairperson's job to initiate discussion, keep it moving, and discourage any one member from monopolizing the discussion. Members were required to listen carefully to one another, yet had the right to dissent and think independently. We wrote the rules on large chart paper and posted them for ready reference.

My elementary students had chosen their own groups. I found that students do not last long in groups in which members do not share reading interests, even if they are best friends. Readers' Workshops became, for my elementary students, a lodestone for social and self awareness. Sally, a soft-spoken and sensitive child, said:

"You get to know other people's feelings when you work with someone you might not know very well."

Jodie, one of Sally's group, added:

"Doing Readers' Workshop makes me learn about myself as well.... Through someone's opinion, I can learn a lot about what she is feeling, and sometimes it helps me to understand my feelings, too."

And Then...the World of Junior High

Buoyed by the successes I had had using Readers' Workshops with my elementary students, I expected matching enthusiasm from my junior high students. To my dismay, instead of being greeted by universally enthusiastic faces, many of the students met me with defiant stares whose expressions said, "Teach me, if you dare!" But, I was committed to making the classroom a community of shared learning, so I rolled up my sleeves, and went to work.

Some of my junior high students had experienced Readers' Workshops in their elementary schools and I found in these students much less resistance, and a greater willingness to engage in positive, productive group work. For the grade seven students, particularly, fresh from the workshop tradition, the program was natural, and their responses in their journals reflected thoughtful, perceptive reading. Carla, Susan and Kathy read John Steinbeck's *The Red Pony*, and were able to draw a comparison between the character Gitano and a horse, Easter:

Gitano and Easter are both old and getting close to death. When Gitano said, "No good anymore" he was also talking about what he thought of himself.

Nellie and Diane worked together through two novels. They made a critical assessment of one of the characters in *Kidnapping Mr. Tubbs* by Don Schellie.

By the time the second chapter comes around, you can already tell what kind of a person A. J. is. He is very nervous, he's a pessimist, always looking on the dark side of things.

Karen and Connie made a prediction as they began to read *The Cay* by Theodore Taylor.

We predict that the ship will sink. The author gives us clues because he is always talking about boats being sunk and torpedoes.

However, many of my junior high students had not experienced Readers' Workshops before and they were skeptical and hard to please. When I tried to institute the same basic structure with my junior high students that I had found so successful with my elementary students, these reluctant students immediately threw up roadblocks. Despite the varied collection of novels sitting neatly on the classroom bookshelves, they set their jaws when I mentioned reading. Cara said she disliked reading because she read too slowly. Cliff said it took too long to read a whole book. I quickly made sure there were some thin books included in the collection! Jerry, a grade eight student, found it impossible to work in a group. An exception had to be made, and instead of sharing with a group he shared his feelings with me in his journal. He chose the book, *Where the Red Fern Grows* by Wilson Rawls. He said it was a book he had always wanted to read, and he became hooked at the beginning:

> When Mr. Rawls goes back to his memories in the Ozark mountains, I feel happiness because life is so slow and peaceful. It gives me a very warm feeling.

Maybe when Jerry tackles a Readers' Workshop again, he will have more confidence in sharing his views with his classmates.

I found all my junior high students — enthused and reluctant readers alike — to be powder kegs of emotion, exploding with doubts and questions about themselves and their world. I felt they would all benefit most from the sharing aspect of Readers' Workshops, being able to find their reading "soul mates" and through sharing with them to grow in confidence and social and self awareness. Still, I worried when Jackson and James, both sporadic workers at best, chose each other as reading partners. My fears were dispelled with their first response to *The Grizzly* by Annabel and Edgar Johnson.

> The best part in this chapter was how the author described David's fear of his father, Mark. The author described David's fear of his father by saying things like David had nightmares and whenever he thought of his father the dark image made him shiver in broad daylight.

As their reading continued, Jackson and James began to relate to the character David as if he were a real person:

> I want to talk to David to ask him why he doesn't like to do male bonding things like fishing and camping. I would probably tell him it's good for him to start doing and liking these things. I would also like to ask him what he likes to do.

I felt that through their responses, Jackson and James began to "bond" as well, as they went through the ups and downs of working together.

Ellen and Jane were both serious students who were committed to various "causes." They chose *The Lilies of the Field* by William E. Barrett, a book about a black man helping a group of German nuns build a church in pre-civil rights western America. They wrote some of their most sensitive responses by posing questions for themselves, then answering them:

> What do you think it meant when the novel said that the "idea of freedom moved around in his head?" (page 95)
>
> We believe that it meant that Homer was free, and that no longer would any dark skinned person have to belong to anyone. In the book it also said that "the idea of belonging to someone stirred a racial antagonism in him, and that no negro would belong to anyone again." We believe that he was disturbed by the thought of him "belonging" to someone. To us, it meant that he could finally do what he wished.

In their final responses, Ellen and Jane revealed how the book touched them religiously:

> We believe strongly that God guided Homer to the empty fields where he found the ambitious and lonely nuns. Even though Homer may have not known or ever realized what effect he had on the nuns, Mother Maria and the small community will always be touched by the man named Homer Smith.

It is my conviction that the more often students work with Readers' Workshops, the better they become at the give and take of group work, and at the development of in-depth responses. After two years of experience with Readers' Workshops at the elementary level, for example, Jodie was able to use her reading experiences to enhance her writing:

> I like the concept of reading deeper into books because it helps me understand my writing so I can put more feeling into it….If I have an idea for a story, I sometimes use the lead-ins and questions we use for Readers' Workshop to help me develop my idea….When I'm conferencing stories, I use what I've learned to give suggestions to improve others' stories.

Even the steely-eyed junior high students who most resisted reading softened in their attitudes as they progressed through their Readers' Workshops. Some time after completing the program, I assigned my grade eight class a lengthy story to read. While some complained, Cliff, who previously bemoaned all reading, said, "It's not that long." Martha, who before Readers' Workshop found any excuse not to read, said, "I'm more interested in reading now." She enjoyed group work, making her own responses, and choosing her own reading material. "You want to read what you choose yourself," she said.

One of the things that I like most about teaching is that it doesn't have to be static. I can change schools, grade levels or even teaching styles in my own quest for knowledge and for sharing that knowledge. Readers' Workshops are not static either, being able to be altered in accordance with the resources available, my students' needs, and my own advancing philosophies.

What doesn't change in Readers' Workshops is the freedom to choose what we read, with whom we want to read and sharing that experience with others. Next September, I'll again look forward to the new school year, when I'll meet some familiar faces who have developed into enthusiastic and intelligent readers. I'll also meet some new faces who will challenge me defiantly with — "Teach me, if you dare!" Using Readers' Workshops as one of my tools, I will indeed dare!

 # References

Barrett, William E. 1963. *The Lilies of the Field*. New York, NY: Doubleday.

Johnson, Annabel & Edgar. 1964. *The Grizzly*. New York, NY: Harper & Row, Publishers Inc.

Rawls, Wilson. 1961. *Where the Red Fern Grows*. New York, NY: Doubleday.

Schellie, Don. 1978. *Kidnapping Mr. Tubbs*. New York, NY: Scholastic Inc.

Steinbeck, John. 1945. *The Red Pony*. New York, NY: Viking Press.

Taylor, Theodore. 1969. *The Cay*. New York, NY: The Hearst Corp.

Strategies for Starting Readers' Workshops with Children Experiencing Reading Difficulties

Cheryl A. Lemire has held regular and special education teaching positions, language arts consultancies, and roles as an elementary corrective learning program coordinator and literacy team itinerant teacher. During her most recent work with students with learning difficulties in grades one to six, Ms. Lemire developed this beginning approach to help the students as they started to behave as readers in Readers' Workshops.

Each year I face a similar dilemma: How can I institute a workshop setting where readers confidently choose their own reading material and respond with personal conviction, insight and enthusiasm to the literature they read, when the children I teach all are experiencing difficulty in language arts? Most of my students believe their role as reader is limited to "sounding out" the words on a page. They are unaware of the importance of interacting with the text. They do not realize the importance of their own experiences.

When I first embarked on Readers' Workshops with these children, and as I have each year since, I saw in the children the lack of confidence and the lack of willingness to take the risks needed to bring meaning to print — the very confidence and risk taking required to learn — and I asked myself: Where do I begin?

Knowing that it is so important for these children to be immersed in a "safe" literary atmosphere that builds on their knowledge and expertise and being convinced that Readers' Workshops could provide that environment, I sought to find a way to focus the children's attention on the role of the reader. I needed a way to show my students that their own experiences are highly valued, that they must take an active role in deciding what they read and that they can be in charge of and responsible for their own learning, for I believe, as Don Holdaway writes in *Independence in Reading*, that:

> Children can never become independent unless they accept full responsibility for confirming their own perceptions, and for achieving an accurate and satisfying understanding of what they read. (p. 66)

Reflecting upon the strategies Nancie Atwell suggests in *In the Middle* for initiating a reading workshop and upon my own past work with teachers on reading and writing process, I realized that to be successful the workshop had to provide a **model** of good reading behaviour for students. Teacher modelling thus became the starting point for the workshop and one way of leading my students towards independence.

It is critical to distinguish teacher modelling from informing and demonstrating. **Informing** is the *telling* of what should occur; **demonstrating** is the *showing* of how something should be done. While modelling includes some informing and demonstrating, **modelling** is the *"doing"* of what we want our students to do. It is not a portrayal of the act of reading; it is the true, honest experience of "This is what I do when I read." As such, teacher modelling provides for students an accurate visual/oral image of what constitutes reading. In addition, it gives value to the act of reading, especially for those students who have had little opportunity in their lives to witness the act of reading.

What follows is a description of the initial workshop sessions with my students, their reactions to teacher modelling and their beliefs concerning reading after they had been involved with Readers' Workshop over a number of months.

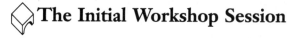 The Initial Workshop Session

Setting Up the Workshop

Often children who are having difficulty reading are overwhelmed by the variety and number of books in the school library and find it difficult to choose the books that will afford them the necessary initial success. Therefore, I begin in one of the following ways:

- having the children choose from a selection of books written by the same author
- having the children choose a book from a selection of reading materials written in the same genre
- having the children choose from a variety of books I have determined they can read successfully

Gradually, as the workshop proceeds, the children will begin to choose their own reading material based on their individual interests and needs.

Choosing an Appropriate Book
To Model Reading Strategies

Often I select a children's book I "love" or I ask my students to select a book they wish to hear.

Preparing for the Modelling Session

For readers who are having difficulty reading it is particularly important to "show it all," to present the *whole* picture of what readers do. Rather than assuming that these students automatically use title and picture cues, for example, to predict the content, I have found that I must think clearly about what reading strategies I might demonstrate explicitly to them. Further, they seem to need more direct attention to the reading strategies that able readers use while reading and/or when they encounter difficulties understanding. In other words, showing them how reading is more than just figuring out the words, that reading begins before the words are encountered, and that it continues in reflective, response activities afterwards are my goals when presenting the whole picture.

One of the books that delights students from ages six to thirteen and that has been most successful for my initial modelling presentation is Janet and Allan Ahlberg's *The Jolly Postman or Other People's Letters*. What follows is a list of possible reading strategies (behaviours) and examples of my matching "think alouds," which are my own thoughts as a reader that I share aloud with the children.

Reading Strategies/ Behaviours I Model	Examples of Possible Teacher "Think Alouds" Using *The Jolly Postman*
1. Title: making predictions about the story content using the story's title	"The main character must be a happy-go-lucky postman who is delivering people's mail. Maybe the story shares some of the letters or mail with us."
2. Book Jacket or Cover: sharing useful information from previous experiences about the author or cover illustration	"Oh, look! There is a cow jumping, a moon holding a letter, a little boy dressed in blue...umm....'The Cow Jumped Over the Moon,' 'Little Boy Blue.' The cover has characters from 'Mother Goose' rhymes. Each of the characters is holding onto letters."

3. Date of Copyright, Publisher, and Author's Dedication: exploring background knowledge and predicting story contents

Opening the book, I comment on the copyright date and other useful information. "This book was first published in 1986 — not long ago — in London, England. I wonder if the story might contain words used by the people in England, words that might be new or unfamiliar to me?"

4. Places in the text where the reader's background experience enhances the understanding of the story

The following connections might be made from the letter titled:
    Mr. V. Bigg
    Mile High House
    Beanstalk Gardens
"Mr. V. Bigg. Beanstalk. Oh, I remember the story of 'Jack and the Beanstalk' and the character of the giant. Maybe V. Bigg might mean *very* big — referring to the giant."

5. Illustrations: sharing thoughts and feelings regarding the quality of the illustrations, the size, colour, line, character expressions, and expressing predictions derived from illustration clues

Many of the letter stamps in this book depict people wearing crowns and addresses that are typical of England so I might make the following reference: "These stamps show a King or Queen on them and one letter is mailed from The Kingdom on May 20. Remember we said the book was published in London, England — perhaps the authors and illustrator are English."

6. Difficult words — modelling the strategy of skipping over a word while reading aloud or of utilizing the story context and/or picture cues to determine the word and its meaning in the text.

I choose words appropriate to my children's level of understanding and for which the story context gives strong cues to the words' meanings.

7. Difficult words — using word analysis strategies to "sound out" a word for which the

I use this strategy with names of people or places: Examples from *The Jolly Postman* might be the

story context is of no assistance	names the author uses — Hobgoblin Managing Supplies, Pickleton, Director, etc.
8. Re-reading — re-reading to make sense	I mark a section of the story and deliberately misread it so that the text does not make sense and then show how I reread the text to make sense.
9. Prediction — wondering what is going to happen, making logical predictions using previous story information to do so	I mark sections in the text where I wonder aloud what will happen next or use previous story infor- mation to make logical predictions.
10. Personal Response — preparing personal reactions to a story — "why I like this book"	I discuss with the students why I like *The Jolly Postman* and which letters particularly interest me.

It is critically important *to prepare to model* **each** of the above strategies and not to overfocus on only one or two of them.

Construction of "My Own Thinking" Signs

I construct "My Own Thinking" signs, like the one illustrated, for myself and for every second child in the group. During my modelling session, I hold up this sign whenever I state what is happening in my mind while I am reading the book to the children. This technique helps the children to distinguish between what I am reading aloud from the text and what I am "thinking" as I read.

Modelling the Strategies While Reading Aloud to the Children

I ask the children to observe closely what I do when I read. As I read to the children I model the "think alouds" I have prepared.

Discussion Time

The children discuss their observations of the modelling and we record their responses on charts. These charts serve both as a reminder and as a reference to the reading strategies the children are to practise. The students also have opportunities in other lessons to add to the charts other reading strategies they know or discover to be useful and successful for themselves as readers.

Practice Time

In partners the children take turns reading orally to each other from the books they chose. Using their "thinking signs" they attempt to do what I did during the modelling session.

Observing the Children

I note which strategies the children utilize and which strategies need reinforcement — that is, which strategies would benefit from more modelling and from mini-lessons — in future sessions.

Additional Workshop Modelling Sessions

During mini-lessons at the start of workshop sessions (see pages 32–42) and with "think alouds," I continue to model and reinforce various reading strategies:

- making predictions using the reader's personal experience
- making predictions using textual information

    I often hold up a "My Predictions" sign, similar to the "My Own Thinking" sign I used above, when I am making my own predictions based on my own experiences or based on what I deduce from the text I am reading.

MY PREDICTIONS

- using my own experiences

- using story information

• responding personally to literature — here again I often make use of a sign — "My Personal Response"

MY PERSONAL RESPONSE

- what I like
- the author's language
- what I wonder
- about the illustrator

When modelling "My Personal Response," I

- share my favourite parts of a book and state why these parts are my favourites
- respond to the quality of the illustrations by discussing drawing techniques and the use of colour or shadings
- respond to the author's use of language and writing techniques; this latter strategy needs to be modelled many times so that the children will carry over this knowledge of the use of language and writing techniques to their own written personal responses

As the year progresses, I encourage the children to discuss whether the teacher modelling and the thinking/predicting/responding signs are useful to them as readers. When I listen to them talk, whether they are in grade two or finishing their sixth year in school, their comments reveal the impact of this process.

Andria: "It [the teacher modelling] helps us understand what you're trying to do for us. Like the thinking. You're telling us what you're thinking in your mind, and you're telling us what you're doing, what you're thinking about a story that you are modelling for us so when we get to the point and when we have to think, we know what to do."

Sean: "It makes you read better."

Tyana: "It makes you understand better."

And Brandie adds:

"We want to try to read the way you read because you know how to read. You set an example."

These children now have the image of what constitutes reading and believe there is a difference between modelling and informing. Listen to the following comments:

Andria: "You're acting it [the reading process] out. You're acting it out! You're not just talking to us, you're acting it out."

Lia continues:

"It helps you more because it shows more than just talking."

Then Andria adds this gem of wisdom:

"Acting is more seeing than just talking and it's more understanding than just talking."

All the children found the "thinking signs" useful at the beginning of the workshop:

Mark: "When you hold it up, you know that you're supposed to be thinking on what you read."

Sean pipes in:

"It starts you off."

Melissa continues:

"Once you see it, you'll always know what to do."

However, as the workshop progressed the children all said that the signs now got in their way and that they were no longer needed. This idea is reflected in Melissa's comment above that they now know what to do — "always."

The children are well on their way to achieving the "independence" Don Holdaway writes about by taking responsibility for their own reading. This progression is reflected in what they express about reading:

Andria: "If something doesn't make sense to you, you go back to the beginning and you start reading back 'cause if it doesn't make sense to you what's the point of going on. You don't understand."

Tanya: "You have to think when you read."

Ian: "A good reader is always thinking about what is happening next."

Amy: "You use your own experiences. In the story that I read, it was like the Christmas story [that] I had known before and the author just used some of that. He put the characters he used in his story and used it as the Christmas story."

Laura: "You have to make sense so other people can understand what it means…"

Brandie concludes:
"Reading is thinking and understanding."

These children are beginning to accept, in Holdaway's terms, the "responsibility for confirming their own perceptions" and are striving for that "accurate and satisfying understanding of what they read."

References

Ahlberg, Janet and Allen. 1986. *The Jolly Postman or Other People's Letters*. London, Eng.: William Heinemann Ltd.

Atwell, Nancie. 1987. *In the Middle: Writing, Reading, and Learning with Adolescents*. Portsmouth, NH: Boynton/Cook Publishers Inc.

Holdaway, Don. 1980. *Independence in Reading*. New South Wales, Australia: Ashton Scholastic.

Parents*: Partners in Literacy

Sandra Wenz draws on her experiences teaching students from their first through fourth years in elementary schools in Kindersley and Regina, Saskatchewan, and in Calgary, Alberta. Ms. Wenz shares her teaching practices through study groups, conference presentations and workshops. Her classroom celebrations are wonderful involvements of children, teachers, parents, guardians and visitors.

Over the past six years, teaching grades two and four, I have become a "parent-watcher" as well as a "child-watcher." Parents and teachers share the common goals of wanting children to be happy in school and to be interested in reading. Readers' Workshops are one way of developing a love of reading in our students. When we connect with our students' parents about what we are doing in our workshops, we encourage and extend the philosophy inherent in Readers' Workshops. By bringing parents into the community of readers, our teaching becomes more effective.

But how can we encourage communication about language learning? What supports can we develop to ensure that the community of readers is extended from Readers' Workshops in the classroom to the home?

For many years curriculum newsletters and parent-teacher conferences have provided some communication between teachers and parents. In an effort to draw my students' parents more effectively and knowledgeably into the world of Readers' Workshops, I have developed a number of additional approaches designed to involve students, parents and teacher to further develop the connections between reading at school and reading at home.

"What did you do in school today?" parents ask, hoping to learn about their child's learning. My dream is that this age-old question is answered by my students telling a story involving themselves and learning. One way I try to make it more likely that my students will share such a story is through the way we do book sharing.

---

*For readers' ease, the word "parents" is used to indicate children's parents, guardians or other primary care-givers.

Book Sharing

I once read that if a child reads an exciting book but can't share it with someone, it's like a solitary fisherman hooking a lunker and having no one to whom to relate the story. In an effort to promote the sharing of books, I established ongoing two-minute book talks to be given by the students. I have found that students are powerful promoters of both books and authors through their two-minute talks. These book talks not only allow the class members to hear about more books and authors, they also provide a meaningful experience in which the students develop both their speaking skills and their images of themselves as readers. The talks also acquaint the students with what their classmates are reading.

Students indicate their intention to share a book by signing a card with their name and the title of the book they are going to talk about and putting the card into a pocket chart near our workshop area. Students take turns leading our book-sharing sessions. The student leader pulls one of the cards from the pocket, invites that student to share, and hands me the card. As well as making an anecdotal comment about the student's presentation in my own evaluation record, I write a positive phrase on the student's card. The student subsequently uses the card as a bookmark for use either at home or at school. I wonder if these bookmarks going home in the hands of the delighted students don't play an important role when parents ask, "What did you do at school today?"

Home Journals

Another tool I use to try to involve parents more closely with what is going on in the child's school day is the home journal. Once a week I have my students write a letter to their families about what they are involved with at school, and in particular about what they are reading. Before they write, the students and I, as a large group, talk about the books we're reading, activities in all curricular areas, our plans, and other happenings at school. The students then individually write their letters to their families in their home journals. That same day they take their journals home where at least one family member responds to the letter. The students keep their journals at home throughout the week to enable them to record some of what they read at home. They note the source(s) of what they read (e.g., book, magazine, newspaper), title(s) of what they read, and whether they read alone, with a partner, or to a partner. When they bring their home journals back to school, I initial their entries. Through this process, the parents are involved in the students' learning and are kept abreast of what their children are reading. I learn how families are responding and encouraging their children.

Daily Reading

We read every day. It is one of our favourite times. Some periods are quiet when we have decided to read alone. Other periods are filled with a buzz as students are grouped and involved in shared reading. At the end of our daily reading the students often discuss their books. They record their comments in their daily reading logs or response journals, often beginning their entries with phrases such as "I wonder," "I think," "I felt," "I predict." This record helps to reinforce the students' learning. As well, the response journals are written evidence to accompany my observations and anecdotal records of the students' interest and willingness to read. At the end of the day many students carry their books home to read, once again bringing what they are reading at school to the notice of their parents.

Shared-novel Experiences

The students gather every day in our story corner to listen as I read a novel. I remember how the novel *How To Become a Perfect Person in Just Three Days* quickly involved my grade four students. I picked the novel because it was fun and because it lent itself to involvement, response, and prediction. Everyone took the book's suggestion for self-improvement and tested the positive effects on behaviour that comes from wearing broccoli! What response! Such wearing apparel and student storytelling going home was more powerful than a note to parents saying, "My teacher reads to me every day." Read-to novels that are of high interest, that encourage talk and that give children joy and enlightenment are important to my reading program and to my efforts to reach out to parents.

Photographs

My class has discovered that pictures really *are* worth a thousand words. During the year, we use photographs to tell the story of reading: reading silently, reading out loud, reading alone, reading in groups, discussing books with peers. I take pictures of reading logs, student book talks, librarian book talks, teacher book talks, storytime, mini-lessons, students choosing novels in the library. Throughout the year I display these pictures in the classroom and on a bulletin board in the hall outside my classroom, along with samples of students' written responses to what they have read and the artwork they have created to illustrate their reading. The photographs celebrate and reinforce the workshop program. They also help the students talk about their work when a parent or other visitor comes for an informal visit. As well, I find the photographs provide an effective education tool during parent-teacher conferences as I can show parents what happens in the classroom when the students read and then write about or discuss their books.

Communication Through Educational Writings

I also use letters home, educational writings, and report card time to foster parent awareness of what we do in our Readers' Workshops. Later in September I send an article to parents that encourages them to continue reading to their child as well as encouraging them to support their child's independent reading.

In the report card folders I include articles to help further explain and foster understanding of the Readers' Workshop philosophy of language learning. Articles from *The Reading Teacher*, published by the International Reading Association, have been particularly effective for this purpose. I also give my explanation of Readers' Workshops in the curriculum letter to parents that accompanies the first-term report cards. Since by the time the first report card goes home, the parents have become aware that their children are choosing quality literature to read and that they read, discuss, respond, illustrate, share and celebrate their novels, Readers' Workshops already have a strong foundation.

As well, I leave a table set up outside the classroom door on which I display the wide range of literature being enjoyed by my students. I also put out educational pamphlets and books explaining different facets of Readers' Workshops that parents who visit can read right there or that they can borrow to take home to read. This lending of reading material promotes interaction, connection, discussion and education about reading.

"Partners in Literacy"

A major link in my attempts to bring parents into the community of readers is my "Partners in Literacy" program. In *Learning To Read*, Margaret Meek affirms that, "To learn to read, children need the attention of one patient adult or an older child, for long enough to read something that pleases them

both. A book, a person, and shared enjoyment; these are the conditions of success" (p. 9). In my "Partners in Literacy" program, I invite parents and other interested adults into the classroom to read, in fall, winter, and/or spring terms. Those adults who have expressed interest as a result of a recruitment letter I send home with my students are invited to join me in a two-hour partners' in-service at the school. The in-service features a slide presentation on how the "Partners in Literacy" program works. The slide presentation is followed by an open discussion about the partners' classroom roles. The in-service establishes the "Partners in Literacy" program purposes: namely, to stimulate student attention and to respond to children's reading in a positive, non-judgmental way. I particularly want the partners to understand their roles as attentive listeners and responders.

Upon completion of the partners' in-service, I assign each volunteer partner four to six students for eight weeks. During these weeks, the partners meet with each of their students once a week for about twenty minutes in the classroom or in some other comfortable area around the school.

Meanwhile, the students plan the books, stories and poems they wish to share with their adult partners. The day before their adult partners visit, the students fill in a reading plan giving their intention to read particular pieces, complete with page numbers. The plan allows the students to focus on reading pieces that they are familiar with so that they can read aloud successfully. It also provides me with a continuous record of the students' progress in choosing and practising reading selections.

The students and their adult partners smile as they become immersed in their books during this special reading time. Many of the "Partners in Literacy" are my students' parents. The adult partners become aware of how children in Readers' Workshops behave like real readers who choose books, read and construct meaning for themselves. These partners learn through their experiences with their student partners that comprehension is extended through talk. They more fully understand how we share our thinking, feelings, and responses to both illustration and text. In addition, by spending this time at school they demonstrate that they are members of a "community of readers." My hope is that this reading and talking together models for parents how they and their children could read together as a family!

Celebrations

My belief that readers need to share and to celebrate their reading has deepened over the years. I believe sharing and celebrating is not only integral to a reader's response to what he or she is reading, it's an extension of it. Self-confidence is developed when students celebrate their achievements at school.

My memories of the end of harvest in Saskatchewan, when our family would gather together to celebrate the completion of summer work with special food, come alive when the members of my class and I celebrate the successful completion of some facet of our reading program. Our celebrations are interactive sharing times where students are leaders in helping to organize and plan events. We invite people who are significant to our classroom: parents, other teachers, school administrators. I make the food; we share our accomplishments. Celebrating what they have accomplished, telling someone about the process involved in their accomplishments, and considering exciting possibilities in their future endeavours all encourage the students to reflect on and to extend their learning. All the activities that make up our celebrations are integral to making parents partners with the children, not just in reading but in all learning.

Producing a video presentation has become an important part of our celebrations. Our videos are prepared ahead of time so that we can show them to the invited visitors. Once, for example, when students had been reading poetry and writing their own, they chose a piece to illustrate and to read for video-taping. With their own art as the backdrop, each student recorded a poem; some discussed the connections between their art and their writing. All of this was done without the immediate pressures of an audience. Once the students and their visitors had viewed all the poems presented together during our celebration, there was a freedom then for the visitors to go to our classroom displays to browse more thoughtfully through the students' works.

We also use video technology to extend the "joining together" of our celebrations to those families who have been unable to attend the celebration by making the videos available for home viewing. Sometimes parents make copies of these "anthologies" of work, and of class members, to be kept as remembrances. One parent took up the idea as a way to keep an ongoing record of his child's school products! Meanwhile, back at school, we can view the videos ourselves, relive the moments, and reflect on the experiences.

At one of our gatherings the students prepared Readers' Theatre productions—dramatic oral readings from novels and stories that the children had adapted as scripts that are then read with the narrators and characters using minimal props and gestures. The parents first joined their children for daily reading, sharing their children's novels and reading logs. This sharing gave the parents insight into how readers respond to their reading, while the Readers' Theatre presentation by groups of students brought parents, students and teacher all into a community of readers. I love how the children stretched themselves to do their very best job.

At another celebration we shared some of the language learning we had gained from working with Caldecott award-winning literature. At the celebration, each student read one of the prize-winning books to a parent or other visitor and explained the art forms of printmaking, collage, and watercolour that the particular Caldecott illustrator had used. The students also read stories they had written in response to *Noah's Ark*, Peter Spier's wordless picture book.

Having parents attend celebrations of the students' reading helps us to show parents much more clearly the aims and methods of Readers' Workshops because their learning is happening in context—with their children at the centre of the learning. The parents go away with a much better understanding of the value of sharing and celebrating reading— basic principles in the philosophy of Readers' Workshops.

One parent responded after attending one of our celebrations with this letter.

Dear Mrs. Wenz:
    John and I would like to thank you and your class for the wonderful celebration yesterday. We really enjoyed being in the classroom and

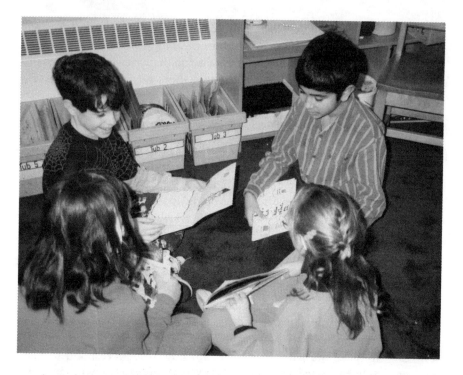

having our son be the leader. What a switch in roles! It's wonderful to see how different language arts is today compared to when we were in school. We've come along way since "Tip and Mitten." Thanks again.

Such letters let me know that celebrations are worthwhile.

Publishing Student Writing

Another way I involve parents in the community of readers is through "books" of students' writings. Each term my students bring one piece of writing to a final draft and publication. Sometimes we publish the students' writings in a class-made book that contains all the students' writings. At other times, each student publishes his or her own work in an individual book. In either case, the writers enjoy attaching a comment page to the book(s) so that their readers can give them feedback on their writing.

The student authors burst with pride as they pack up their published piece of writing in a special envelope to carry home to their family. (If all the students' writings have been published in one book, the students take turns carrying the treasure home.) The students feel great delight bringing their book back when the class gathers as authors with completed pieces to share with one another. As well, they enjoy sharing their family's written comments with their classmates. These comments show the students and me that their parents are being helped to understand the close connection between reading and writing, between home and school, between each of them and me. The parents have no doubts that their children are writers and readers deeply involved in their learning.

Growing Connections with Parents

As the year progressed I felt a growing connection between parents and me and with our common goal of literacy. Listen to some of the parents' support for their children's successes during Readers' Workshops:

—We feel this has been a super program. Julie's reading has improved immensely and we are really pleased with the style of books she has chosen. It's fun to share her excitement. Thanks for all the positive input you give our children.

—Because the program has a social element to it, Somer enjoyed reading. It probably gave her insight into how others reacted to the stories. I think Somer's reading speed has improved, and her vocabulary increased.

—David has enjoyed the reading program very much as well as the opportunity to work cooperatively with other students. I am pleased that David has had an opportunity to read with another child as he usually reads independently.

—This program has greatly improved David's reading confidence. He was always convinced that he couldn't read through the harder chapter books. Peer pressure helped him to stay on task and achieve his goals. He happily reads three chapters in an evening. Before, his home reading was limited to one chapter at a time. He seemed eager to find out "what happens next." Readers' Workshop benefits all the children. However, I feel it is a wonderful way to encourage reluctant readers to take the next step in reading levels.

—At the beginning of the school year Christine had difficulty getting involved with her books. She laboured through chapters when she had to and seldom completed an entire book. During Readers' Workshop, she has caught an excitement of books and an enthusiasm to read. She has completed two novels with her friends and is enjoying a third. She reads early in the morning, at noon, and/or before bed. Having a friend to encourage her through the odd tedious chapter, a friend to laugh or cry with as they read together, has added tremendously to Christine's literary skills. It is a very worthwhile program, and both my daughters would like to see it run twice a year.

Becoming a "parent-watcher" as well as a "child-watcher" has led me to notice activities that may have been influenced and encouraged at least in part by the parents' awareness of Readers' Workshops and how they work in my classroom. As the year progressed, parents were quick to visit the public library to borrow a copy of a novel in order to help us have enough copies for our Readers' Workshop groupings. Two moms arranged a visit by their children to a local bookstore to meet author Kit Pearson because their children's Readers' Workshop group was enjoying a novel by Pearson. Parents became more flexible and supportive in arranging for reading groups to complete projects such as plays and puppet shows at home. Parents purchased books for their children in response to titles and authors requested by their children. The number of parents volunteering for "Partners in Literacy" increased as the year progressed. The parents' support for our publishing house at school steadily increased as our stories and books were shared at home.

Seeing how parents have responded to my efforts to involve them meaningfully has led me to automatically plan for ways to let them know what we are studying or reading, what projects are being done, what authors are interesting to their children, or what ways they can help in school. I am rewarded by their willingness to tell me exactly how their children are responding to my program and growing within it.

References

Cross, Susan, et al. 1989. "Partners in Literacy." *Literacy Bulletin*. Calgary, AB: Calgary Board of Education. October.

Manes, Stephen. 1983. *How To Become a Perfect Person*. New York, NY: Bantam Skylark.

Meek, Margaret. 1982. *Learning To Read*. London, Eng.: The Bodley Head.

Spier, Peter. 1977. *Noah's Ark*. Garden City, NY: Doubleday.

Reflections on Process

"What Have You Done to My Child?"

Wendy Chamberlain and Debbie Huitema began using a literature-based reading program a few years ago when they taught year three and six students respectively. Despite being in different classrooms, they worked collaboratively to develop their ideas and programs. In the past three years they have served as valuable in-service resource people for teachers, librarians, parents and administrators.

"What have you done to my child?"

I wondered what I had done and responded by cautiously asking for clarification.

"What do you mean?"
"My daughter has started reading in every spare moment at home. She's been carrying this book around and is always talking about the story. If I can't find her, she's on her bed with her nose in a book."

It was the third week in September and already we were getting positive feedback in each of our parent/guardian-teacher conferences. We were thrilled that our new reading program was motivating children to read.

Thinking back, it's difficult to remember exactly how we got started on our new program, but we do both remember feeling dissatisfied with the reading component of our language arts program. In June at the end of the last school year our language arts consultant suggested some literature that she believed we might find helpful in planning for our next year's grade three and grade six classes. Early in the summer we each read *In the Middle* by Nancie Atwell, *The Art of Teaching Writing* by Lucy McCormick Calkins and *Whole Language: Theory in Use* by Judith Newman. Then we got together and collaborated.

As we talked about what we liked about the three books, we began to think about what would work for us, what we needed to change for our particular students, and how we would start making those changes. This talk enabled us to put into our own words our beliefs about how people read and what might be necessary for our revised reading program. These beliefs emerged for us:

- students require regular and frequent time for reading
- students should be provided with the opportunity to choose their own reading material
- students need the opportunity to communicate about what they read
- students need the chance to take ownership for their learning by setting and evaluating their own reading goals
- students need to be taught strategies that good readers use

We could hardly wait for September when we could begin to implement our new ideas. We spent the rest of the summer in used bookstores and at garage sales collecting books for our class libraries. We learned a lot about children's books and became very concerned about our choices. What do students like to read? What reading levels should we purchase? What topics will the students be interested in? What is good literature? In the past, we had not focused at length on what the students' specific reading interests were. Thinking of our students over previous years, we realized that, although we knew some were reading avidly on their own, we did not know what their specific reading interests were, and, worse still, we were not part of their reading lives. We were "teaching" our students reading but we weren't reading *with them*. We wanted to know what they liked to read and what level of material they were reading so we could build on their interests and strengths.

We started to develop our own literature base. We each read children's

books and our knowledge began to increase. We were able to list qualities we liked in books and we found new and interesting authors. In trying to provide for a wide range of reading levels in our classrooms we found that there were numerous novels that could be read by students in grades three or six. When choosing books we were now able to help each other make appropriate choices.

We spent September helping the students become interested and involved in our literature-based reading program. Students in groups of three or four were choosing books that interested them from our class libraries. We forced ourselves to overcome our instincts to push certain books and let the students make their own choices. Each group of students was given class time to read, discuss and write about their books. And each group set daily reading goals. We soon noticed changes in our students and in the classroom atmosphere.

During reading time, students were so involved in their books that we had difficulty stopping reading time because they did not want to put their books down. They wanted to finish the page or chapter just as adult readers do. On days when our reading schedule was disrupted students complained that their reading time was lost. Reading was becoming an activity they looked forward to and valued as important.

The early morning conversations in the classroom had changed from events of the previous night and television gossip to what the students read the night before in the books they had taken home. We often overheard their comments:

> "I was so worried when Fern's father had the axe in his hand."
> "I didn't like the way *The Cartoonist* ended."
> "Did you finish your reading goal last night?"

We realized that the children were truly growing in the literature-rich environment we provided when they began to try to hide new books in the classroom library so they could have the first chance at signing them out.

During individual conferences with students, many students admitted to choosing and enjoying books that they wouldn't normally have chosen. Even some of our good readers had only been reading one type of novel such as science fiction or mysteries. With their group's encouragement, they have become involved in reading a wider variety of novels.

Class surveys we had given on the first day in September indicated that many students had read five or less novels the previous year. By the end of September, most students had already surpassed their previous year's total. Throughout the year we monitored students' monthly reading goals and noted the progressive increase in the quantity of books read. Five books quickly increased to ten and even fifty per month.

Students were setting daily reading goals for themselves that were greater than we had anticipated. They had started to challenge themselves by increasing the amount they were reading and the difficulty of the books they were choosing.

Other positive feedback came early in the year from parents. They shared with us that telephone conversations about books were common. Books were being read at the breakfast table. In one particular group of boys, if one of the group had forgotten to take his copy of the book home, one of the others would cycle over to his home with a copy to read. The grade three girls had sleep-over parties where talking about their group novel was part of the evening's activities. Parents were joking with their children that maybe they should be watching some television.

We were delighted. As their teachers, we too had noticed these changes in our students.

Our next step was to evaluate:

> Had the students' reading actually improved?
> What did the students think of the program?

Like many teachers, our classes had children with a wide range of reading levels. Throughout the year we recorded marked improvement in all students on vocabulary and comprehension on standardized tests. The improvement was significantly greater than what we had experienced in the past. In addition, the students exhibited much more confidence when approaching these tests.

We held individual reading evaluation conferences with our students where they expressed their feelings about the program and what affect it had had on them. The students told about changes in their attitude towards reading and in their reading habits. Comments like the following were common:

> "Before reading workshop, I used to only read comics."
> "Reading workshop helps me write good stories and learn new words."
> "I'm more confident and I read faster."
> "I used to read only thin books."
> "I've read more books this year than I have in my entire life."
> "I like to read because you can learn from your book."

The improvement on test scores confirmed our belief in the program, but what was more meaningful to us was seeing our students viewing themselves as effective and lifelong readers. Our students viewed us as readers too, because we were enthusiastic and shared our love of literature with them.

Our greatest resource was each other. Although we taught different grades in different areas of the school, we met on a regular basis to share successes and concerns. We found this time invaluable as we solved problems and worked on improving our programs. When we read professional literature, our frequent meetings gave us an opportunity to reflect on and discuss how the information gained could benefit us.

We are constantly building on our knowledge base through reading, seminars and classroom experiences and we have formed a study group with other colleagues to share and reflect on our classroom practices and experiences. We continue to grow along with our students.

References

Atwell, Nancie. 1987. *In the Middle: Writing, Reading and Learning with Adolescents.* Portsmouth, NH: Boynton/Cook Publishers Inc.

Calkins, Lucy McCormick. 1986. *The Art of Teaching Writing.* Portsmouth, NH: Heinemann Educational Books, Inc.

Newman, Judith. 1985. *Whole Language: Theory in Use.* Portsmouth, NH: Heinemann Educational Books, Inc.

Who Says Junior High Students Don't Want To Read?

Brian Adams writes from his recent experience teaching students in grades eight and nine. With eighteen years of teaching experience, some of it with special education students from ages six to sixteen, Mr. Adams also draws on his interest in helping students to overcome their reluctance and disinterest in learning. Mr. Adams is committed to workshop approaches in reading and writing.

Stomach-wretching laughter filled the library during our first Readers' Workshop session as Rob, a self-confessed grade nine nonreader, rolled onto his side and grabbed his response journal. His laughter, interspersed with bouts of talking to himself about his book, *One Fat Summer* by Robert Lipsyte, continued. The class watched in silence as Rob scribbled in his journal, rolled over again, picked up his novel and continued to read.

"Thanks, Rob, you've just made my day," I said.

Offended, he replied, "I didn't do anything. What are you picking on me for?" You see, Rob had been unaware of his outburst. He had been so involved in his reading that he was unaware of the wonderful lesson his "disturbance" had demonstrated—that everyone, including reluctant readers, can get enjoyment from books.

Rob was a nonreader, but a nonreader by choice. When I told him that there was no option in the workshop, that he had to read, he guffawed at the idea. When I told him and the rest of the students in the class that they would have some choice in the books they read, parental consent pending, I got the obvious questions and suspicious remarks:

"You mean I can read anything I want?"
"You're going to let me read Stephen King in class?"
"V. C. Andrews is OK to read?"
"You're not going to make me read your books?"

Some students thought this freedom of choice was great. Others, including Rob, were not convinced that I was really going to give them considerable freedom to choose their own books. Again obvious questions came:

"If we choose different books, how are you going to ask us questions?"
"How long do we have to finish the book?"

"How are we going to do the test at the end?"

They were surprised by answers that seemed radical to them. In fact, I wouldn't be giving them comprehension questions they *had to* answer when they finished their books!! We then talked about quantity and quality of response journal entries.

Rob still wasn't convinced. He didn't know any good books. Any good authors. And he didn't seem too interested in finding any. That's where, in my mind anyway, one of the most important and effective aspects of being a language arts teacher comes into play. I took Rob to the bookshelves. "Here Rob. I've got just the book for you. You are going to love this. I remember laughing out loud when I read this book. You'll finish it in no time." Skepticism on Rob's part. You bet. But I had done something he wasn't used to. Not only had I recommended a book to him, I took him to it. And I told him that he was going to enjoy it. I gave him a book I had read, one I had enjoyed, one I knew he would enjoy. It fit Rob. I matched the student to the book.

In my Readers' Workshop Rob became a reader. So did others. But in order to initiate such changes in students' reading habits, we need to make changes in the way we teach our language classes. For me the elements of teacher responsibility, time to read, ownership of reading, and classroom practice are the focus for making such changes.

Teacher Responsibility

Matching students to books becomes a key for Readers' Workshops at the junior high level. As teachers we must have extensive knowledge of what books are out there, of what books will hook our students. We have to know our students and we have to use that knowledge to match them with books we think they will enjoy. When students ask for recommendations we have to have them. So, most of my reading now is young adult literature.

I fill my room with books. Lots of books — different authors, different genres, different reading levels. Students see that books are important to me as soon as they walk into my room. I make them important. Books are visible, and they see me reading all the time — before class, in the halls during class change, at lunch hour. I stop students in the hall, students I don't teach, students I don't know and ask them about their books, and I ask them for recommendations about books to buy and then I buy them. I ask to read books I haven't read when the students have finished reading them. The message the students receive is powerful and succinct — books are important!

In my workshops, I model reading. I share with my students the reading that I do. As Donald Graves writes in *Writing: Teachers & Children at Work*, "Reading different authors…provides different voices and topics for children to sample" (p. 29). If we truly believe that children become better readers by reading and better writers by reading, then we can't shrug off our responsibility to engage students with a variety of authors, styles and genres. The objective isn't to turn students into the next Hemingway, Cormier or Korman; the objective is to have students experience the benefits of language and to gain insights and ideas for their own reading and writing. Students, consciously and subconsciously, copy authors' styles, diction and how the authors treat elements such as conflict and plot structure. Once students have used these styles, diction, and elements in their own writing, they become theirs. They become "theirs because they choose and experiment on their own" (Graves, p. 30).

The entries students write in their response journals show that their reading does indeed provide them with ideas and background information that they use in their own writings:

Dear Chris,
    What are you going to write about when we write stories? I'm writing about Viet Nam. Myers has inspired me and some day I, maybe, can write like him.

Adam

Or Charissa's entry:

You know, when Mr. Adams first talked about Historical Fiction I thought it was just about medieval stuff. Now when I read novels such as *Underground to Canada* and *The Hand of Robin Squires* it just slams me in the back of my head like fireballs, about how little I thought about the cruel ties of society." (Charissa — grade eight)

There is a world of literature out there that students have not yet explored and part of our job as educators is to provide students with opportunities to explore in these areas.

 ## Time To Read

Using Readers' Workshops demands that we practising teachers make some radical changes in the way we teach. Gone are the days of turning the page in the teacher's manual to find out what skill we are to teach to the entire class next; gone is the scope and sequence chart and gone too is the sense of security those items provide. In *When Writers Read* Jane Hansen suggests that the ideal reading teacher is a teacher who loves to read and can't resist books, a teacher who accepts the responsibility for helping children learn to make decisions about their reading, a teacher who respects and responds to what students already know (p. 159). Teaching reading to students means teaching what the students need, when they need it, in the context of their own reading.

With this philosophy in mind, I cast aside the traditional once-a-week booking into the library for free reading. For me, once a week wasn't enough time to foster the new priorities for reading that Nancie Atwell talks about in her book *In the Middle*, priorities that include fluency in reading, initiative, involvement with the text, pleasure in reading and appreciation of literature.

I want my students to be readers, and to perceive themselves as readers. In order to do this I give them time to read. John Goodlad in 1984 found that junior high school students spent less than 3% of their time in school reading; in high school they spent less than 2% of their time (Atwell 1987, p. 156). If students are nonreaders in school they are certainly not going to be readers outside of school...unless we encourage reading. Give students time to read and you get positive results:

During the past two weeks of Readers' Workshop, I have found myself reading an obscene number of novels. So far I've completed four 200 or more page novels. I've enjoyed them all. (Jocelyn)

Giving students time to read in school also provides motivation for students to read at home:

What also surprised me was that instead of watching TV, I was reading for more than two hours a night. I find myself wanting to read more and more. (Brad)

I used to hate reading and only read books when I had to (like for a book report) but now I enjoy reading and I think that is because you got me into the habit of reading more. (Tammy)

I'm starting to recognize good books from poor books. It's really amazing because I didn't read that much last year and now I want to read this year. (Curtis)

 # Ownership of Reading

I try to read all of the books recommended to me by my students, but I end up abandoning many of them. They're not books I want to read and if I had to finish them I'm afraid I would have the same negative attitude towards reading that some of our students have today. Yet, if we truly want students to read we must give them what is rightfully theirs — ownership of their reading. Indeed, one of the most important things we need not only to understand but to implement in our classrooms is that right of ownership and the self-selection of books. To do this, however, does not mean that we can't offer suggestions, make recommendations, and gently guide students towards better writing. After some gentle guidance, I have students who have devoured Dick Francis novels and others who comment:

I can't believe I read the Hardy boys at the beginning of the year. My favourite author now is W. O. Mitchell. Thanks for putting me onto him. (Jeff)

In two weeks of reading I've turned from a nonreader to an Agatha Christie lover. (Noam)

When I was reading *Fallen Angels* I couldn't put it down. I even read on the bus and trust me, I don't usually do that. (Marc)

 # Classroom Practices

Modelling reading and sharing reading play major roles in my classroom. When my students spend two weeks reading, I read too. Reading in Readers' Workshop is not a "Do as I say, not what I do" activity. I can't tell my students to read and then spend my time marking papers, reading response journals or planning the next unit. That double-edged sword doesn't fit. Reading with my students is a priceless teaching activity. So is the sharing of both the young adult and adult literature I read. Students share what they read as well. The more we read and talk about the books we read, the easier it is to talk about them. One book reminds us of another and one author reminds us of other authors. So my students and I devote the last period of every week during Readers' Workshop sessions to "student share." The students come to class prepared to share a selection, from a paragraph to a page in length, that, for whatever reason, they find intriguing or enjoyable. In doing so they "sell" books to their peers. *One Fat Summer* was on reserve from the time Rob laughed aloud in class until the end of the school year. Students recommending books to one another is a sure-fire way of getting students reading. When students are given choice of books and are exposed to a wide sampling of authors and story lines, they become more personally involved in the reading and demand even more time for reading. This change in involvement includes the poor and the reluctant reader!

> This is coming from a guy that hated to read at the beginning of the year and thought books were the worst things in the world. Now I don't mind reading. I'm actually reading at home for enjoyment without anyone forcing me to. (John)
> Today I actually read at lunch and on the bus and was happy to do so. (Brad)
> Last term when we had to read Historical Fiction I was one of the people who groaned. To my surprise the books that I've enjoyed the most are Historical Fiction. Since the beginning of reading workshop term I've read 14 books. (Terry)
> This year I've read and finished more books than I ever had in my life. I've read 15 books this school year and I'm still going. (Kevin)
> This year is different. I actually read the whole book through. I even read on my free time or right before going to bed. (Susan)

As a teacher, the decision to change the teaching of reading from a "traditional" approach to a workshop approach is personal. But, more and more, we know that the fundamental way to learn about teaching reading and writing is to read and write ourselves. As Jane Hansen writes, if we are able to say, "Yes, I read," and "Yes, I write," then that allows us to say, "Yes, I teach reading," and "Yes, I teach writing."

Because I take time to read with my students and I share ownership for book selection and responding with them, my Readers' Workshops "disturb" them all — interrupting their reluctance to read. Like Rob's "disturbance" of the class when his spontaneous laughter interrupted us, these are positive disturbances! For me they demonstrate the power in being able to choose what you will read.

Who says junior high students don't want to read?

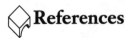

References

Atwell, Nancie. 1987. *In the Middle: Writing, Reading, and Learning with Adolescents*. Portsmouth, NH: Boynton/Cook Publishers Inc.

Clark, Joan. 1981. *The Hand of Robin Squires*. Toronto, ON: Irwin Publishing.

Graves, Donald H. 1983. *Writing: Teachers & Children at Work*. Portsmouth, NH: Heinemann Educational Books, Inc.

Hansen, Jane. 1987. *When Writers Read*. Portsmouth, NH: Heinemann Educational Books, Inc.

Lipsyte, Robert. 1977. *One Fat Summer*. Toronto, ON: Bantam Books.

Smucker, Barbara. 1977. *Underground to Canada*. Toronto, ON: Puffin Books.

So How Come We Aren't Doing Questions in This Class?

Marian R. Hood has taught English and drama in Calgary for the past thirteen years. She has presented workshops and led professional development days for various groups of Alberta teachers. Ms. Hood is a published poet and co-edits a literary magazine of poetry, fiction and art.

When the students in my English classes came in this past September I felt a little like I was standing before them in my underwear. I didn't have my semester planned; I hardly had the first week planned! But I was determined to try to implement a Readers' Workshop approach similar to the one Nancie Atwell describes in *In the Middle*. After reading *In the Middle* at the end of last summer I approached Victoria Conrad (see next article, pages 132–139), who taught across the hall from me, with Atwell's ideas and together we decided what we thought would work with our particular students and planned strategies for implementing Readers' Workshops in our classes.

I decided not to teach my classes a novel this year and to use the time I would ordinarily have spent teaching the novel for Readers' Workshops. In each of my classes students would spend one period a week reading novels they selected and writing letters in their response journals or literature logs about those novels. I chose Friday for my Readers' Workshop classes. (It's taken me twelve years to get smart about how to handle Friday classes!)

As I set about restructuring all my classes, I was somewhat uneasy about using a Readers' Workshop approach with my students in the grade twelve academic stream. If I let these students read anything they wanted would they be prepared for the provincial final exam at the end of the year? Somehow I couldn't picture a marker being thrilled by a major response on Danielle Steele or Sidney Sheldon. I compromised by asking my grade twelve students to read at least three novels during the semester: one from a list of books I compiled, one novel written by a Canadian, and one other.

In the junior courses I varied the pattern somewhat. I asked my students in the grade eleven academic stream to read at least two novels, one by a Canadian author and one from a list of books I compiled, while I asked my students in the grade ten general stream to read at least one novel from a list I compiled. There were novels by Canadian authors on all three of my lists.

The students could complete their minimum reading requirements at any point in the semester. However, regardless of how many books the students had read they were still expected to be doing one of three things during every Readers' Workshop: reading a novel or full-length work of nonfiction, writing about their reading in their own literature logs (lit. logs), or responding to other students' letters in their lit. logs. The plan worked quite well for my grade eleven and twelve students. My students in the grade ten general stream, however, found a full period of reading too long so we began each class with a fifteen-minute Readers' Workshop before we went on to other English activities such as writing and/or reading and discussing pieces of literature together.

The first semester of Readers' Workshops and lit. logs were challenging for both me and the students. We all had to do a fair amount of rethinking and adjust what we were used to doing in the classroom. Both the students and I had to adapt to the fact that not everyone in the class was reading the same novel and that I did not have a set of chapter-end questions I would be asking all the students to answer. In their lit. logs the students were encouraged to quote passages they particularly liked, react to the characters and to situations in the book, predict what might happen next, ask questions, speculate about what the writer was up to and why, write down memories from their own lives that helped them understand the book, and evaluate the book in relation to similar books they had read.

As well as having my students respond to their reading in their lit. logs, I asked them to write two literary letters, that is, letters about the literature they were reading, a week to someone in their class and to write to me once every two weeks. When the students wrote to one another they were writing to people they knew and chose to write to. As a result their writing had a purpose other than to please the teacher.

Through their lit. logs and their literary letters the students were encouraged to take control of their own learning. They decided what was important in a book. If they had questions they could ask someone in the class for answers or they could write questions down thereby putting them on hold until they had read further. The communities of student readers began to function like the community of adult readers to which I belong. They recommended books to one another and each class developed a favourite book, largely because students wrote to one another and sparked one another's interest.

Most students were easily committed to using their logs and writing their letters. But I found that even reluctant writers eventually came to explore meaning through writing. Because the writing in the logs and letters was exploratory I wasn't concerned with technical correctness. Once students realized I wasn't going to dock marks for technical errors, they tended to write more and, in some cases, the mechanics began to improve.

I came to enjoy the letters my students wrote me. Kelly, a student in the grade ten general stream, wrote a letter almost every day. One of the first books he read was *Deathwatch* by Robb White.

> Miss Hood
>   This Madec guy in my book is crazy!! he is going to make Ben take off all his clothes or he is going to shoot him. I don't understand how the dead man got shot in the neck also as well as in the ribs the bullit in his neck was a different bullit than the one in his ribs so how did that happen. this is a pretty good story but hard to understand in some spots. I still think Madec is a looney though I think Ben should kill him and save himself the agony of wandering around the desert naked!!
> Kelly

Darret was in Kelly's class and decided to read *Deathwatch* after hearing Kelly talk about it.

> Dear Ms. Hood,
>   I cant put *Death Watch* down. I keep reading it in class and miss everything you say, but I will be dane it by the end of the week. Ben is

really smart but kind of luchy two. He just barly made it to the water hold, I feel sory for *Ben*, it makes me happy to think I dant have to go threw such pain and torcher. As for *Madec* I wish he was dead. I hope *Madec* makes a mistake soon so Ben can live.

Later on Darret expressed his frustration with the lack of happy endings in the books he had been reading. This time his book is *Far from Home*.

Dear Ms. Hood,

All my predictions are rong, Im in the last pages of the book and the lady with the baby went back to her husband, The Buckley Arms has been sold, Toms wife killed her baby and had a miscarriage and everyone is fighting. This is the thered book I've read this year that ended in an unhappy way and Ive only read three books! I want to find a happy book.

Darret

Perhaps my favourite example of commitment to the Readers' Workshop came from Chris, also a student in the grade ten general stream.

Dear Ms. Hood

I have just started book three. [Chris was reading a science fiction decology at this point.] so far it is really boring. I sure hope that this book gets better. After the two previous, and excelent books this one looks like it might kill the series. I got the series for Christmas, and surprised my parents very much because I appreciated the books just as much as I did my NINTENDO.

While I think Chris had always liked books, Darryl surprised himself.

Miss Hood im now reading rumble fish and it is an excilent book. im half way throw the book Monday and should be finished next week and this will be the fourth book so far. i grade 7, 8, 9, i had a problem with sitting down and reading but know im going great gun's what book are you reading? what's it about so far?

Darryl

Nevertheless, not everyone took to the literature logs immediately. Some students continued to be unsure of what I wanted and others said that answering set questions at the end of each chapter of the novel they were reading would be easier. I guess, in a sense, they were right, but what I saw in the lit. logs was students asking their own questions and approaching text with a sense of wonder. I wasn't willing to give that up. We lived with the discomfort of moving away from the familiar. As students did catch on to how to use their lit. logs, there was a dramatic change in the tone of their writing about literature. Perhaps the most striking example came from Thuan, a student in the grade twelve academic stream for whom English is a second language. Here he writes about *The Chosen* by Chaim Potok.

As I continue to read from half way of chapter 1 to the end of chapter 2, the novel gets more and more emotional. At the beginning of the ball game to the end, it seems to be rather a war that both teams try to win. Ironically to what the members of Reuven's team and including himself perceive with the unimpressive feel towards the jeshiva team at the way they play in the first couple innings, they, the players of the jestiva team, or the antagonists at this point of the novel little by little come back and win the ball game after Reuven has to quit because he got hit by the baseball into his left eye from Danny Saunders' bat.

In this excerpt Thuan uses literary terms but I had the feeling that he wasn't really engaged with the text. In my comment to him I asked that he write to a specific person about what he was reading and his reactions to it. I also suggested a couple of other students who were reading the same novel and that he might like to correspond about the book with them. His next letter, addressed to me, begins quite differently.

To Miss Hood,
   You're right. My question about whether or not Danny hit the ball deliberately to Reuven was answered when Danny come to visits Reuven in the second time, one day after he suffers all the anger Reuven threw at him…. At this point in the novel, I'm aware that both Reuven and Danny coincidentally love reading. You wouldn't believe this but Danny said he reads about seven or eight books a week outside of his schoolwork! I found this hard to believe but it's true.

In both of these letters I see Thuan thinking about the content of the novel. The second letter is less formal and Thuan seems to be taking more risks. He has begun to acknowledge his personal responses to what he is reading.
   I wanted all my students to have a place where they could be tentative, as all readers are, without feeling that they would be penalized, and I hoped that their lit. logs would prove a good place for this sense of safety to grow. And as the students became more comfortable with their lit. logs they did begin to take greater risks and to explore their reading in more depth. Thuan, for example, began to reflect on his choices of reading material and on his reasons for deciding to read what he did. He began to evaluate his reading and to set goals for himself.

The reason why I have chosen *Death Planet* is because I like to take a close look at different style of writing from the literature that I've read so far in this course. However, this certainly is not the first time I have an idea to attempt reading this "action adventure," but this time, my goal is to learn along as I read and hopefully, it would help me more in terms of writing and comprehension in the future. Honestly in reading, my biggest problem's trying to imagine and visualize the exact picture in my mind, therefore, as far as I'm concerned, if I don't get a good hold of this, I might continue to face part of the failures in English.

Equally important, reading is supposed to be fun, enjoyable and recreational. Thus, I have seen the point. Every book I had read contains unique and interesting elements of both the writing technique and the story itself as well.

The exchanges between students in the logs were polite and supportive. Three grade twelve students descended on the public library and took out copies of *The Handmaid's Tale* by Margaret Atwood so that they could read it together. Many interesting letters went back and forth as the girls worked their way to a common understanding. At times they asked me for help; at times they answered one anothers' questions. Sometimes they gently corrected one another when they thought one of them had misread a passage. They understood that reading is an act of faith: trust the writer and the novel will eventually make sense. The following exchange comes from Kim's log.

Dear Kyla,

It is going to be a bit hard to write to you and not give anything away since I am further into the book *The Handmaid's Tale* than you are. I found the first chapter and part of the second very odd because I didn't know what was going on. It sounded to me that they were in some kind of prison which it turned out to be sort of true, having no rights & all the confining rules. I also found it confusing at first, the way the writer jumped from what was happening in the "present" to things that happened in the "past." It was necessary though because it is the "past" sections that explain the background so the "present" parts make sense. It explains why things have happened and how things got to be the way they were. While the format was confusing at first I think it is an interesting format and enjoyed it. There is one section where the narrator describes Nick in great detail and it is one of my predictions that something is going to happen between the two of them. All the while when I'm reading I keep wondering what it was that turned the society into what it is and that isn't revealed until much later in the book. Some parts when she is remembering about Luke I found uninteresting and kind of boring and I think that was because I was so anxious to find out what the great tribulation was that caused this society to take the shape it has. Another prediction that I want to make is that Moira who appears so far only in the past is going to resurface. I think this because she is talked about so much and the narrator keeps remarking how she wishes she could see her or find her. I wasn't sure what to expect concerning how the handmaids got pregnant and it was kind of what I thought but didn't believe any society would permit it and the way they carried out "The Ceremony" was even more surprising. Well I will end this letter now and hope that you will write back very soon.

Kim

Dear Kim,

I was really surprised by your comment that in the beginning you thought they were in some kind of a prison. I never thought of it that way until you mentioned it. I just figured that they were in a gymnasium. You put a different light on it for me. I, too, had some trouble trying to make sense of the style of writing. The way the author jumped back and forth made it quite confusing for me. Though now as I have read further into the novel I understand it more and realize that it is a very effective way of writing. The predictions you make caught me a little off guard. I never thought that something would happen between Nick and the narrator because that is forbidden and by what I have read I didn't think the narrator would ever do anything that she wasn't supposed to. Especially after the incident that happened in the doctor's office (chapter 11) She then had the chance to bear a child but she denied it because it was against all the rules. So I guess I'll have to keep an open mind about this prediction of yours. I also agree with you about some parts with Luke being boring. Though to some extent I found them also intriguing. I want to know more about what role he plays in the narrator's life. I feel that later on he may return. I had a little difficulty believing the handmaid's role in life. How can they just be there to bear children for the commander's family. I hope as I read on I may get better understanding of this process. I have not come to "The Ceremony" part yet so, I have "no comment" on it.

Kyla

Harry also read *The Handmaid's Tale* and, although he did not correspond with the three girls, he had some of the same concerns about the book.

Dear Ms. Hood,

I finished *The Handmaid's Tale* during the holidays and actually ended up enjoying the book. Although it is still a little disappointing not to really find out what happened to her. In the end the talk by the doctor who found the tapes really pulled the whole thing together. Its a good thing Margaret Atwood put it there because there were still things I didn't pull together until the end.

It's so frustrating to see the society from outside because we see all the corruption that's going on and how much everyone hates the situation and yet goes along with it. Why don't they get together and change it...

There were many examples in the logs of students clearly being caught up in their books. Maria tended to be quiet and serious about her studies. She tried *The Stone Angel* by Margaret Laurence, and abandoned it in favour of *Who Has Seen the Wind*. Here she notes some of her reactions.

> Dear Kolbi,
> It seems to me that the farmers are not having much success with their crops. I find that the farmers are very tense in trying to better their situation. I can't believe that Mr. Candy was so unreasonable about helping the farmers out. I quivered when I read that the Ben had been visited by bot-flies in his ear. I could feel his pain! I felt sorry for Mr. Digby when he proposed to Miss Thompson and she did not except. I was also not surprised when Mr. Powelly visited Mr. Digby and suggested that the Ben go to reform school. I think the Ben's character is quite bad.
> Happy reading
>
> Maria

Some students took longer than others to become accustomed to lit. logs instead of content questions, and there was frustration. But most students were willing to persevere.

> Ms. Hood
> Hi. I'm happy to hear my lit. logs are improving. I think I'm finally catching on....

As with any other teaching techniques, for a few of the students the lit. logs never did work well. Sometimes Dave wrote about books; sometimes he didn't. Even when he didn't write, the knowledge that he should be needled him a bit. He chose to write letters to himself.

> Dear Dave
> Well its Christmas and that means lots of skiing and drinking, I have given my book a little rest for a while because I am too excited about skiing and drink. It will leave my system after I get drunk and ski for a day or five.
>
> Merry Christmas

When I polled my classes at the end of the first semester every single student who answered my questionnaire said that he or she would prefer to choose his or her own novel rather than have everyone in the class study the same novel. Some students took the time to write me saying that I should keep the Readers' Workshop going in the next semester.

> Dear Ms. Hood,
> Well, this is the last lit. log entry.
> I would first like to say that even though I have struggled through reading books (minimal time) I think that the   reading portion of

English is really important. Our reading periods have also given me
that last moment of a stressful weak to wind down....

Shae Lynn

Dear Ms. Hood,
   I know I just wrote to you but I thought my last letter should be
to you.... At first I wasn't too keen on the idea of Lit. Logs because
I more enjoy reading just to enjoy the book. I think it was good
though because it helped me look at the mechanics and how the author
uses different ways of writing style more critically. I've learned more
about writing through reading, does that make sense? I thank you for
your help in interpreting some of the things I didn't understand in
literature. I enjoyed this semester.

Kim

I decided to continue Readers' Workshop in the second semester. The
second semester has in many ways been easier. I can now, for example, give
clearer instructions to my students about what I want them to do in their lit.
logs. However, one area that I still need to do a lot of work on is evaluation.
Students put a good deal of time and effort into the logs and that effort
should be reflected in the mark that goes home. In the first semester I had
tried an evaluation scale that took descriptive terms from the curriculum
guide. I developed a five-point scale (weak 1 2 3 4 5 strong) with unwieldy
descriptors such as "an increasing ability to articulate thoughts and feelings
about reading material," and pointedly clear ones such as "willingness to
respond to literature in literary letters at least twice a week."
   As I attempted to use the scale during the semester I found it didn't
work all that well because the students had trouble making the connection
between what they were doing and what I was rating on the scale. A couple
of students were quite upset with their marks and used their lit. logs to tell
me so.

Ms. Hood,
   I must admit I am very disappointed in my mark in lit. log. Usually if
I get a mark like this and I deserve it, I try much harder and take more
responsibility. Although this mark I don't think I deserve. Although I
cannot do anything about it was very discouraging and I have never
been put down by a teacher by such a terrible mark. Now you have
made me feel incapable and very unsure. I am sorry but I have missed
alot of time but they are all excuse with that I think you were wrong
in concluding my mark.

I was pleased that the student felt comfortable enough to tackle her
disappointment in a letter. We talked; she went back to the guidelines and
steered away from simply retelling the plot in letter after letter. Her mark

at the end of the course improved and she was satisfied that she hadn't been treated unfairly. Meanwhile I continued to revise the scale for future semesters. My revisions grew out of my discussions with the students, my growing awareness of what is happening in my Readers' Workshops, and my curricular goals. New items appeared such as "demonstrates the use of personal experience in understanding the literature," while others disappeared. My observations and my ways of tracking them are still evolving.

Since I stood nervously before my class last September I have worn out several pens. I have a long list of books recommended by students to read. I have grown to know my students through their logs. Some students have figured out that, in fact, questions are still essential to understanding what they are reading, but the questions now are theirs, not mine. Some students who didn't see themselves as readers now do. I am learning how to minimize the confusion and insecurity for students creating lit. logs for the first time. I enjoy hearing from my students and appreciate their patience as I search for words to describe to them what they are doing.

Next fall when I meet new students I will not feel like I'm standing in my underwear. I will look forward to exploring the world of literature and learning with my students and I will hope that any students who ask why we don't do questions in this class will find their own answers.

 References

Atwell, Nancie. 1987. *In the Middle: Writing, Reading, and Learning with Adolescents.* Portsmouth, NH: Boynton/Cook Publishers Inc.

Atwood, Margaret. 1985. *The Handmaid's Tale.* Toronto, ON: McClelland & Stewart.

Laurence, Margaret. 1968. *The Stone Angel.* Toronto, ON: McClelland & Stewart.

Mitchell, W. O. 1947. *Who Has Seen the Wind.* Toronto, ON: Macmillan of Canada.

Potok, Chaim. 1982. *The Chosen.* New York, NY: Ballantine Books.

Sebestyen, O. 1980. *Far from Home.* Boston, MA: Dell Publishing.

White, Robb. 1972. *Deathwatch.* Toronto, ON: Dell Publishing.

Big Dividends: Andrew's Story

Victoria Conrad taught grades ten through twelve in the same English department with Marian Hood when this piece emerged from her experience with a grade ten class. She has adapted the practices she developed then to influence her current work with groups of fifteen- to seventeen-year-old students, mostly boys, who have "dropped out" of junior high school. They now want back into school yet need to build up their basic skills in order to move into high school settings. She reports that it is exciting to watch her so-called nonreaders curl up with a novel for thirty minutes every day! Ms. Conrad says she has taught high school English "forever," belying the freshness with which she takes on new projects and new ways of thinking.

Marian is generally a quiet sort. Reserved, almost. Bounding about, waving books is not her usual style. Yet there she was early in September, completely under the spell of this Nancie Atwell, and sounding frenzied. She had my attention.

Journal writing where the students delve into their thoughts regarding a novel they are reading? Sounded exciting. I wrestled the book away from Marian, and a few weeks later, I too initiated a new reading-writing program with a motley crew of grade ten students.

I began with some uncertainty, for my plans to give time over to "just reading" were in conflict with my needs to "cover the curriculum" in a half-year semester — a semester that had an exam at the end. Somehow I had to make the workshop fit in alongside the other activities I had developed to meet program goals. Nevertheless, as a reader myself, I felt that if I were successful in turning my grade ten students into readers they would be better able to handle the English program requirements. Would the change to a workshop prove worth while?

I began my journey in the library. I had asked our librarian to talk about a variety of Canadian authors since we needed to read at least one Canadian novel, and to include an enormous reading range. Christine did a splendid job, and by the end of the period, each student had chosen a novel.

Next day, back in our classroom, we began with fifteen to twenty minutes of silent reading. I played classical music or environmental tapes, and each day politely declined the use of Tony's tapes. I read too. A lovely sane way to begin each class. During that first week of our Readers' Workshop, I also spent time reading to my students excerpts from letters I had written to Marian (see pages 122–131) in my own journal in which I shared with her my thoughts and questions about what I was reading. I also read some excerpts from Marian's letters to me about her reading. Encouraged by my example, the students slowly began to write in their journals several times a week as I'd requested. The importance I placed upon reading and upon responding to that reading soon became obvious, without me having to give the usual "sales talks."

"Hey, Mrs. C., we gonna do this every day?"

"Yes, Chrystal, we are."

On Fridays the students had a choice of reading for the entire period or of writing in their novel journals, which they handed in at the end of that period. On the initial Friday, I silently offered up a prayer to Nancie Atwell, as I slid a Vivaldi tape into my ghetto blaster, and sat down to write to Marian. Thirty-two assorted teenagers, last class on a Friday afternoon, soft music. The wonderful sound of turning pages, writing. Could this last? Hindsight tells me that the relative ease with which these routines were established was due in part to the tone Marian and I established for the students, and the respect and openness that was present in our journals to each other. Much modelling. This was **Serious, Important Stuff.**

The quiet reading and writing did last, and I came to love those relaxed, quietly productive Fridays. The students' first responses were cautious, somewhat vague, and usually not much more than a page. They were highly respectful, perhaps because each letter began "Dear Mrs. Conrad," thereby pinpointing their audience as this nicely eccentric old lady.

I gently nudged them into thinking more deeply about the literature as I responded to their letters, and, as Marian has said, eventually they began to turn into READERS. Some of them more so than others, of course. This transformation into readers in itself was great. Happy-ever-after-endings. But I found even greater satisfaction in the unexpected side effects. Little things, mostly, like what happened with Andrew.

Andrew's family had come to Calgary when he was four or five. Vietnamese, very western in his dress, but shy in my class, Andrew knew English was his weakest subject. He knew too that sooner or later I would discover that fact. Probably sooner, because I'd done a battery of pre-tests with this class — everything from reading comprehension to creative writing — and Andrew's scores were all low. His first letter reflected his apprehension, as he politely said things he thought I would like to hear:

October 13

Dear Mrs. Conrad,

As you probably know, it has been awhile since I read a book. To me I never liked reading until the last couple of weeks when I found out reading could be so enjoyable. Right now, I started reading a book called "Dreamspeaker." I liked this book a lot because its very dramatic and its heart breaking....

Keep in touch!

Andrew

Achieving a sense of safety for the students so that they would feel secure enough to explore their feelings about what they were reading and to share the results of their explorations was one of my hidden goals. Dare to take a risk, chance being wrong, admit to not understanding parts of your novels...and gradually the students did begin to expose themselves. Andrew writes in a later letter:

Dear Mrs. Conrad,

I have read your comments to my question and to tell you the truth, things really made sense to me now! Before, when I was reading the first few chapters, I didn't quite understand what Peter was unfocused off, and when I can't understand something about my character, my mind sometimes wandered off into deep space of somewhere miles away.

That's why, when I read a story, I can't seem to get myself more involve into the character or the story itself. But now, with more understanding about Peter, I was able to focus better to the story...

On October 27 I received a three-page letter. It ended:

...My predictions of the ending wasn't what I thought it would be. I thought Peter would live happily with the old indian without the police finding him, but my predictions turned out to be the opposite way. Worst of all, I found the ending very shocking and it wasn't close to what I predicted.

Keep in touch!

Andrew

Dear Andrew,

Well, you truly are discovering what a novel journal is all about. I could almost HEAR you thinking (click...click...click...) on these past few pages. Congratulations! I must confess the ending startled me too. Peter appeared to be progressing so well, and changing, too. I guess I still tend to want things to be "nice" — that's not very realistic, is it?

When I reread the final three chapters, I could sense what was coming. Foreshadowing galore. Poor lonely scared Peter. Poor everybody who feels alone.

Sincerely,
Mrs. C.

The Andrews of the world, reserved, anxious to do well academically, are so often afraid to approach teachers. But my kinship with Andrew had been established. The teacher felt the same way he did. Well, well. Keep in touch. (The teacher was also manipulative enough to slide in technical terms, so she didn't have to lecture much! Shameful.)

The respectful tone in the students' letters was now beginning to spill over into other classroom interactions. Our school had come to expect much inappropriate behaviour from the first semester crop of grade ten students, but with this class I experienced very little...especially after I started to encourage them to write to one another for variety. They were quickly gaining respect for their peers as readers, writers, and as "people."

October 27

Dear Kevin,

The book I have just finished reading is called "Dreamspeaker," a novel written by Cam Hubert. This book is about Peter, a character which reminded me of Doodle. ("The Scarlet Ibis"). I say this because Peter and Doodle both struggle from their disabilities...I liked this book and I would recommend it to readers because it is very descriptive with lots of details, and how Peter handled his problems was fascinating. So, if you're looking for a book to read, I highly recommended you to read this book called Dreamspeaker.

Keep in touch!

Andrew

Andrew surprised me when he chose to write to Kevin, who was also a bit of a loner in the group. Kevin was a quiet boy and a STUDENT. He didn't exactly fit into this group of young people, either, but I had never seen the two boys interacting — thus my interest in the unusual "connection."

Kevin's journal entries had wowed me from the first week. His first novel choice was *World of Wonders* by Robertson Davies. His lengthy journal entries had been soundly analytical, and, he made constant personal connections throughout his reading. He was teaching himself. I just stood on the sidelines, applauded and occasionally tossed a question at him. Here's a taste of Kevin, an excerpt from a five-page letter from October 20:

...I think this [a quote he had just inserted] conveys the whole feeling of the fair: stereotypical, prejudiced, cheap looking, made to look important and showy. Another descriptive statement by Magnus is about the back alley lights of the theatre that he plays in while he is travelling through western Canada with a theatre production company. This is very interesting, because it gives the flavour of small rural towns in a relatively young and fresh country. Magnus states: "You knew where you were heading because the only light in the alley was one naked electric bulb, stuck laterally into a socket above the door, with a wire guard around it. It was not the placing of the stage door that surprised me, but the fact, that for me, that desolate and dirty entry was always cloaked in romance." (p. 260) This showed me that Magnus was becoming more dramatic and sensitive, as well as being an intelligent and observant realist. It also shows how the author is descriptive in his writing. The fact that this quote reveals that Magnus is becoming more of a romantic, and, more likely more caring too, brings me to another question you asked....

So, when Kevin received Andrew's letter, I suspect he was as surprised as I was.

Dear Andrew,
    The book you have read sounds excellent. When I read in your letter that the main character reminded you of Doodle, you had my attention right away. I liked the character of Doodle a great deal, and if the main character of this book is anything like that of Doodle, then this book is for me.
    The book that I have just finished, *World of Wonders* by Robertson Davies, was very descriptive too, and the main character, Magnus, was also fascinating in the way which he handled his problems. I like that in the book that I read, and this book sounds very similar. For those reasons I am very interested in this book. I just may read it.
                                                                    From Kevin

I expected that Kevin's polite response would mark the end of the boys' tentative relationship. Wrong, again. (I encouraged my class consistently to make predictions about their characters and plot happenings as they read!)
    In November, I tried a new approach. The entire class would read the same novel, *The Chrysalids*, and perhaps have more incentive to write to one another. They didn't (unless I pushed it) but other things began to happen. Andrew again, following a page of chatting about how sci-fi books help him to be more creative, and how the cover drawing had reminded him of a recurring childhood dream:

...After reading the book a little, I found the first few chapters a bit confusing because I didn't get what the author was saying. Thin I got Kevin to explain it to me and now I understand more clearer of what happened in the first few chapters...

...After understanding more about David, I found him to be alone, scared of what's going to happen, and not being able to talk to his parents without getting yelled at. I sometimes get yelled at by my brothers because of something I did wrong, or something I forgot to do. I'm almost like David because I don't go to my parents to talk about my problems. I mostly go to a best friend or uncle....

Until next journal entry,
Keep in touch!

Andrew

I have omitted a large section where Andrew spoke openly about going to his uncle, and how glad he was that David had Uncle Axel to talk to. I felt a sense of Andrew now, one that I would not have had through the usual classroom assignments, and certainly not in discussions, because Andrew never did talk in class. Only in my seminar groups with tea and cookies, when groups of students would gather to discuss with me the results of their independent work in other parts of our program, did Andrew make tentative offerings.

Andrew was beginning to approach Kevin whenever I suggested that working in twos and threes might be a good way to tackle a current assignment; also I saw his face light up when I posted my Seminar Group Lists, and he and Kevin were both in the SEALANDER group. Occasionally I would spot them trotting down the hallway together, chatting, undoubtedly about their current novels!

Here's Andrew in early December, sounding much more confident: he had just completed *The Chrysalids* and we were both proud.... *The Chrysalids* is a difficult read for a youngster who only spoke English when he was away from home:

...One other thing which I thought was instrumental in their successful escape was that they cooperate and worked as a team. I think team work is very important because in recent years I have joined a lot of sports and group work and I found out that many minds put together are better than one. That's why David's groups are very successful because they worked together to help one another. Here's a statement "We are the New People — your kind of people. We're the people who are going to build a new kind of world — different from the Old People's World, and from the savages."

To end this journal entry, I would like to tell you that I really enjoy reading this book a lot. Also, I'm glad I finished it by the deadline.

Keep in touch!

Andrew

And I had thought this youngster to be non-academic material! Oh, and he used the term "foreshadowing" earlier in this letter. (Just thought I'd toss that in!)

In December Andrew read *Hunter in the Dark* (his choice) and *Arsenic and Old Lace* (my choice and another full-class read). With *Hunter*, he elaborated upon his relationship with his parents, and was very hard on Mike's parents, whom he felt were too harsh with their son. The way Andrew ended his letter changed. "This is the writer signing off." And he had indeed become a "writer." His voice was becoming stronger; he was beginning to add much more personal detail and was connecting to his readings, becoming more involved in them. He was less afraid of appearing vulnerable, and apparently, less concerned with what I would think.

In mid-December I received a letter about *Arsenic and Old Lace*. This time Andrew had correctly underlined the title. Kevin had reminded him! He compared this play to *Romeo and Juliet*, and felt Shakespeare's characters were "much, much smarter." He discussed black comedy, with difficulty: because of his background, this light play was harder for Andrew than a Shakespearean drama.

And then, this mid-section that endeared Andrew to me forever!

> I think the most craziest character in the play is Teddy. He is a kind of character that is insane and amusing. I find him very challenging because he is too wild. I don't think I could ever act like him as you probably know. People thinks I'm too shy to do anything wild like that, and I'm too untalkative. It's some of the fears I hate having and I'll do anything to be like Teddy (almost anything) wild and creative.
>
> He speaks as he wants to without feeling shy about it and has a very interesting side which I could never release from me. If I could, I would be a new person having one side of wild and the other side of me, just me.

This program did eat into class time that I had once used to keep us busy covering all the content I'd felt we had to do. But using the time differently paid big dividends. My students became readers. The atmosphere within this classroom became notably more positive as the students learned to respect themselves and one another as readers. There was a frequent exchange of novels and much book talk throughout the semester. Many students were dazzled that they had actually read three books, my minimum request. Others read as many as ten books. But for me, the biggest gift was what I learned from this class regarding the final period on Friday afternoons. I didn't have to "control" students who had real and important things to do and say. Mozart...ocean waves...pages turning...pens rushing across journal pages.... Pure sanity. Right, Andrew?

References

Hubert, Cam. 1978. *Dreamspeaker*. Toronto, ON: Clarke, Irwin & Company Limited.

Davies, Robertson. 1975. *World of Wonders*. Toronto, ON: Macmillan of Canada.

Wyndham, John. 1955, 1975. *The Chrysalids*. London, Eng.: Michael Joseph.

Hughes, Monica. 1982. *Hunter in the Dark*. Toronto, ON: General Paperbacks.

Kesselring, Joseph. 1968. *Arsenic and Old Lace*. New York, NY: Dramatists Play Service.

One Student Connects—Meaning Is Made: Jason's Story

In this piece a teacher and her student jointly explore personal response and meaning-making, a foundation stone of all forms of Readers' Workshops. Within the constraints of a fixed grade twelve curriculum readers' response journals promote the process of exploring, sharing and communicating new meanings. **Kathleen Weir** *has taught English at both junior and senior high school levels. Her own explorations of reader response have been over the last few years, a long way from her early memories of teaching in a resource room with reading kits! Ms. Weir's student,* **Jason Summach**, *from her grade twelve class, is currently at the University of Calgary.*

Before my students and I used writing and reader response journals in my classroom, each assignment I gave my students was an end in itself. The assignments may have involved questions and pre-writing activities but they were set by my agenda. Even when I allowed my students a choice in topics for writing, the choices were based on what *I* wanted the students to explore and discover.

Then, after much reading and discussion with colleagues, I decided to use one tool of Readers' Workshops, the readers' response journal, with my classes, and my life as a teacher and the lives of my students changed dramatically. As I began to use response journals with my students and I began to see the potential that lay within their pages, I was forced to re-examine what I do as a teacher. I was forced to open myself up to what my students are learning and *how* they are learning, and to consider how I can best effectively nurture the possibilities that exist because of the students' explorations into knowledge.

Journals have now become essential to my teaching, for it is through the journals that I have been allowed a glimpse into the thinking of each of my students, that I have been allowed to glimpse how they learn. As Jason, one of my grade twelve students, wrote in the introduction to his essay on *The Handmaid's Tale* by Margaret Atwood:

> The human mind is an organizer, not only recording the passage of events, but also analyzing and synthesizing those memories for further examination. Details of our lives that seem trivial at the instant may resurface much later as part of a new realization.

The response journal is an ideal vehicle to help students organize, analyze and synthesize. It allows them to make connections, to explore and to grow, and it allows me an opportunity to watch closely that process of growth and learning. I join my colleagues in elementary and junior high schools who also find their students' journals reveal growth and learning.

I read and reply to my students' journals throughout the semester, and then at the end of the semester I collect the journals again and read through them from beginning to end. And so it is as I sift through a semester's worth of Jason's work in his writing file and reader response journal, that patterns of thought emerge. I notice things I hadn't noticed before. I see, not only the finished product in essay form, but the half-formed thoughts along the way as Jason works to make meaning. As Jason himself wrote about his journal in his final journal evaluation:

> Just a note about my journal — it is a *living record* of my feelings for the last five months. It contains my changing attitudes, personal highlights and tragedies and has become very dear to me.

I found the seeds for the paths Jason's thinking was to follow early in his journal in this response to the story "Youth" by Joseph Conrad:

> I find it very frustrating to lose track of my memories — I wish I could be rational enough to *really* remember my feelings and experiences…. People, feelings, and other memories sit in my mind; slowly, bit by bit, they get replaced by other feelings and images. Soon, what I remember may be similar to what really happened — but it is a re-creation, not the real thing.

This comment was in response to the class discussion of the various layers in the story "Youth." We have what happened, we have what Marlow recalls (his memories of what happened), and we have what the narrator recalls Marlow recalling. As Jason points out in his journal:

> You could even add another layer; that which the reader remembers or feels. Then again, that is true of any story.

When I first read this entry in Jason's journal, I barely gave it a second glance — it didn't even warrant a check mark. It was not until I came back to it much later, when the semester was over, that I realized its significance. Things were beginning to happen for Jason here. He was sorting out some ideas that would come together in his final essay of the semester. At about this time, Jason began reading *The Handmaid's Tale*. In one of his responses he writes:

> First of all, the last part of Amazing Grace goes, "was blind (not 'bound'), but now I see (not 'am free')." I suppose this is an example of how memories get superimposed with other memories, experiences or ideas.

And later:

> "This is a reconstruction. All of it is a reconstruction." "That is a reconstruction too." — This is how this chapter begins and ends. I think Offred's mind is sharp enough to get the events and conversations right, but her feelings 'at the time' may be obscured.
>
> …
>
> It is neat to see her superimposing her murderous feelings into the situation with the commander. She claims that she didn't feel that way, yet that is how she remembers it. Interesting.

I, too, am interested. The idea of "reconstruction" has captured Jason's attention and it is hard for him to let it go. He sees it *everywhere*. Upon reading "Memories of Christmas" by Dylan Thomas, he writes:

> This seems to be a reconstruction too. How could Thomas remember who said what, and what carol they sang…? His perceptions must have been somewhat affected by the Christmases he has had since then.

I waited for Jason's essay on the *The Handmaid's Tale*. It was not forthcoming. The program of studies pushed us on to *Hamlet* and for the next six weeks Jason's mind and heart were engaged elsewhere—or so I thought. The following excerpts from Jason's *Hamlet* essay proved otherwise:

> What is happening on stage isn't real, but it 'appears' to be: therefore, the audience accepts it as reality.
>
> …
>
> Shakespeare's major statement is that the purpose of acting is to somehow capture a piece of reality and present it as if it were a mirrored reflection of that reality. However, he doesn't limit theaters to the reconstruction of factual events.
>
> …
>
> There are many other forms of 'mirrors' besides theater through which a piece of reality is captured.

During this period of time Jason also wrote the poem "The Crystal":

> A master in his craft
> can create
> feelings
> in the hearts of another,
> in some cases,
> the work is so powerful
> that it overrides everything
> that filled the heart
> in the moment before
> the shared experience
> between artist and audience
>
> …
>
> The sediments may be lost
> or washed away over time.
> But, in some cases,
> the crystal stays anchored
> and draws other particles to itself.
> Experiences that share the heart
> bond to the grain
> of an artist's inspiration.
> Soon the crystal lies at the center
> of a larger image of itself,
> composed of everything that is real
> to the touched.

My comments in response to Jason's essay on *Hamlet* and his poem were as follows:

As I wait for the Atwood piece, I see reflections of Atwood in each of these last two pieces you have written. "Mirrored reflection of reality," "reconstruction," "mirrors...through which...reality can be captured." All of these point to Atwood. Art, drama, the act of writing itself—shaping our thoughts and feelings into something that will touch or be understood by another, is a given. Art exists to organize human experience....

Finally, it came, the essay I had waited for. The following is an excerpt from Jason's essay on *The Handmaid's Tale*:

...Offred, in Atwood's *The Handmaid's Tale*, finds herself caught in a tangle of trying to figure out what is real as synthesized by her own mind. Swept along by the current of Gilead the past has become a field of possibilities that she is forced to sort through....

Besides being a fascinating observation in relation to money, the passage offers some interesting hints as to why memory becomes fractured or distorted. As time passes, experiences are deposited throughout one's being, some adding strength and density to the interior of one's beliefs and others forming on the surface, offering the potential for a new direction of growth. It seems that memories enter into a sorting process by which a storage area is chosen. A catalyst for memory is the vehicle by which the memory attains value and direction. That is, something makes our experience stand out in order for it to be remembered, and it is what stood out that will bring the experience to memory. The other details linked with that experience are often overshadowed or forgotten. The fact that these details are missing offers the brain a number of possibilities to choose from in 'filling in the blanks.' For Offred, her desperation for something to hold onto gives each of these possibilities great value, so much value, in fact, that she cannot tell which one is real. The pain and pressure that she has endured has somehow fractured her reality into larger possibilities rather than the usual 'detail-sized' possibilities. She needs something to hold onto, so she can either choose one possible past and accept the future it will motivate her towards, or she can throw all of the possibilities away and continue to drift, but Offred keeps her options open by believing all of the alternatives presented to her....

In its entirety, Jason's essay is a masterpiece. It is intelligent, thoughtful and beautifully written. In the language of the essay Jason himself reconstructs the ideas that he had been exploring in less formal responses to other literature and that he had poetically constructed in "The Crystal." But what strikes me as being perhaps even more important than the finished product is the process that was involved and the learning that took place en route to the final product. Jason himself described some of that process:

The largest impact on my writing has been the concept of "reconstructions." I reconstruct the feelings or ideas that I have into an essay or poem that will be broken down and reconstructed by the reader. This…is a pretty a good indication of where my writing [thinking] has led me.

The response journal is a powerful tool in any classroom that values individual thinking in the making of meaning. I know that the journal is central to Readers' Workshops at all levels because it gives such an impetus to individuals' own meaning-making explorations. As Jason's journey shows, using a journal provides a personal forum that allows students to make connections and to synthesize their ideas; it makes it possible for them to review their thinking and to draw conclusions; and it makes it possible for them to look back and follow the steps in their own learning.

Learning is a very private thing. Students do not learn because or even when we want them to. Coming to know what we know may occur at times and places distances apart. The seeds that develop into that knowledge may occur when we are least aware and then blossom unexpectedly. The process that produces that end product is to be revered, respected and given plenty of breathing space. And we must provide a safe place in which this process of making meaning can evolve. Readers' Workshops and the response journal offer such a place.

References

Atwood, Margaret. 1985. *The Handmaid's Tale*. Toronto, ON: McClelland & Stewart.

Summach, Jason. 1989. Work completed during English 30. Calgary, AB. Unpublished.

Reconsidering the Response Journal

Margaret H. Hajdu decided to try workshop approaches to reading and writing with her grades eight and nine classes after reading Nancie Atwell's In the Middle. *She is a teacher with over eighteen years' experience in public and alternate schooling.*

The lifeblood of Readers' Workshops is the response journal. During the first mini-lessons that I give my grade eight students as they start out in our Readers' Workshop, I stress the importance of beginning and maintaining a response journal. I encourage them to make regular entries, in the form of letters, and ask them to hand their journals in at least once every two weeks so that I may read their responses to their books, and when appropriate, respond back to them. In addition to the "letters" they write to me in their journals or literature logs, I encourage them to write to friends and to share with one another their thoughts and feelings about the books they are reading.

As I read the students' journals I often come across entries that contain interesting insights into the books they are reading, into the process of reading, or into their own abilities to respond. I photocopy these entries (with permission from the authors), make overhead transparencies, and use them in mini-lessons to illustrate the kinds of responses I hope to find in their journals.

The students respond positively to the apparent informality of the workshop and to the lack of what they perceive as structure. However, the structure is there, provided by the mini-lessons and imposed by the questions, comments, and "gentle nudgings" I give them towards reaching a deeper understanding of the text, or of the process of reading. The response journal becomes the central learning tool of our Readers' Workshop.

Because a dialogue is established between me and each student, the teaching that takes place is specific to the student's interests and needs. We start our discussions with what the student knows and move towards a deeper understanding. We start with the skills the student has and build on them. When the students come to recognize that they have something worthwhile to say about books they are validated as readers and they assume ownership for their reading and for their growth as readers. As one student wrote:

> The part that I looked forward to was the comments at the end of the paragraph I wrote. Some of them were very inspirational. I like this method [journal writing] a lot more than just writing about the book, but actually being able to criticize the book.

But getting students to the point where they are really reflecting on the text or on the reading process is not easy. Initial responses frequently tend towards plot summaries. That is not to say that there is no value to re-telling the plot. For meaningful response and reflection on the literature to evolve, an understanding of the plot is essential. Nevertheless, some students are reluctant to leave the security of re-telling plot. It is hard to convince them that they have opinions and ideas that are worth sharing, or that once they attempt to share their ideas, their personal utterances will be accepted.

During the first year that I tried Readers' Workshop, I mentioned the frustration I was feeling to a colleague, Barb Wallace (see pages 44–47), and she recommended that I read Toby Fulwiler's *The Journal Book*. Since Barb was the same person who had introduced me to *In the Middle* by Nancie Atwell, the book that had given me the courage to start a Readers' Workshop in the first place, I gratefully accepted her loan of Fulwiler's book.

One of many good ideas I got from this book was the suggestion that students reread their journals at the end of the year, make a table of contents, and then write a final entry evaluating the quality of their own responses. In that final response they have to select their most favourite and their least favourite entry and give reasons for their choices.

At the end of that first year of workshop I had my students do exactly that. I was astounded at the insights they achieved. It was through this activity that I discovered first hand what a powerful tool for learning response journals can be. The students learned more about responding to literature and reading by doing this simple exercise than they had by listening to a whole year of my repeated mini-lessons about what made an interesting entry. In some cases they were far more critical of their own efforts than I would ever be:

> As I sit here and look over my previous entries I noticed that my entries on the books I read were poorly written. They were very general and very undone I left alot of loose ends and I really didn't tell much about the author. My favourite entry was the one I did on my analogy of life being like a bike ride it was more thoughtfully done and had meaning to it.

This student expressed a real sense of disappointment in what he had done in parts of his journal but he was also able to commend himself on an entry that went beyond the text, his "analogy" of life.

Rather than disappointment, some students expressed a real frustration with themselves and the journal entries they had made:

> The journal with the least impact was *Lucky*. I thought my journal entry rambled on and on and never really told me anything. It certainly wasn't very interesting and I found myself wanting to quit reading it. When I do read it [the journal] I usually find myself *feeling* about the book or characters, what I thought when I was actually reading it. But I didn't remember anything. It reminded [me] of a bad episode of "Dynasty." This journal entry did not help or interest me at all.

Although she was frustrated with some of her entries, this student was able to go on and recognize the strengths of some of the responses in her journal, to achieve a balanced view of what she had accomplished:

> The journal entry that had the greatest impact on me was the one on *Marjorie Morningstar*. This book had such a simple plot but I realized it had many sub plots. When I read it [the journal] again it brought back how I *felt* when I was reading the book...the entries reminded me of how I felt when I was reading, I wanted to shake Marjorie and tell her what to do. You wanted to be her friend and by reading that entry I remember that.

I'm not sure why this student underlined the words "feeling" and "felt" in her entries. It may reflect the strength of the emotion she felt, or perhaps, she was trying to signal me that she was meeting my expectations of what a journal response should contain.

This exercise of reconsidering their journal entries after ten months of response also afforded an opportunity for students to see their own growth as readers. In those months, they discovered, they had grown up. Their entries began to reflect this new maturity:

> As I read back I notice that towards the end I start to read between the lines; maybe I have matured. In fact I know I have.

By reflecting on past journal entries, the students began to appreciate what they had learned, to see value in it and to take pride in their accomplishments.

> I have developed new ways of comparing authors. For example, in entry #20 I compare the author of *The Omen*, with the author of *The Chrysalids*.

Another student wrote:

> My best journal entries...deal with foreshadowing analysis, an area which I feel I'm fairly good at. I think that being able to analyze foreshadowing is a concept that could be useful in future reading.

Another insight some students gained, through doing this exercise of reconsidering their journals, was related to their patterns of response. Through numerous mini-lessons I had presented a variety of types of responses. Some mini-lessons had focused on personal response, linking literature to one's own life, while others had attempted to look at responses that included literary elements, beyond plot summaries. Most mini-lessons naturally related to the process of responding to the literature, but some encouraged students to reflect on how they were reading — predicting, anticipating, re-reading, getting caught up or being bored. I encouraged students to attempt each of these types of response, and their ability to do so was reflected in the mark they received for the quality of their entries. The students' abilities to recognize their own patterns of response enabled them to move towards providing the variety I was hoping to see in their journals:

> One pattern I found in my writing was that I always write about my feelings. Very rarely do I relate a book with personal experience...it [journal writing] records feelings and thoughts you might not have again.

This student has recognized the fact that his entries tend to follow one pattern of response, while also recognizing that one of the greatest values of the journal is that it is a record of "feelings and thoughts you might not have again."

Another student discovered that she had attempted a wide variety of responses:

> I always start a paragraph with 'what makes this story...,' trying to figure out why the author wrote or chose to display his characters in a certain way. I also realized a pattern in that I always like to know or say what I learned from reading a book. I am also analyzing why something happened in a book. Foreshadowing and how or why the author did something was another thing I noticed a lot in my writing.

The review process also allowed for incidental learning. Some students discovered things about themselves, for themselves. For example, all my admonishments to students to keep their journals intact would not have the same impact as this student's own realization:

> I think writing journals has made me realize I have responsibilities. I look back at my journal and I laugh, I can actually remember writing every one. But, then I see how many are missing, its kind of

disappointing to me but it has taught me something that I feel I have carried through to all my classes.

As I read my students' reconsiderations at the end of that first year of workshop, I marvelled at the insights they had gained about reading, literature, and their own journeys as learners. It occurred to me that it was a shame that those insights were coming at the end of the year, when the immediate opportunity to improve the quality of their responses had passed.

So the following year I resolved to introduce the exercise at mid-term rather than waiting until June. I hoped that by reconsidering their responses from September to January, the students might use what they learned from their re-evaluation to discover ways of improving their journals throughout the rest of the school year. By the end of January the students' journals contained a sufficient number of entries and a sufficient variety of responses to make reconsideration of the journals worthwhile. To increase the sample of entries, I had encouraged the students to share their journals in small groups. (Some sharing had been going on all along when the students exchanged journals to write one another letters.) I asked the groups to come to a consensus about what characteristics they thought made an interesting entry as opposed to the characteristics that made a boring one.

Their self-evaluations of journal entries showed that at mid-term they could determine the same strengths and weaknesses as my students had at the end of the year before. They, too, felt that what was general or rambling or incomplete was superseded by responses that were aesthetic, personal, and thoughtful, as well as by entries about literary elements.

By having the students go through this reflective process in January, and having them write a reconsideration of their past entries at that time, the students and I were able to see marked growth during the rest of the school year in the quality of their entries. They, and I, had used their own entries, guided by the content of my mini-lessons in the workshop, to determine the depth of their thinking and learning. By reconsidering their response journals during the school year they'd renewed their commitment to using the journals, and I had renewed my belief once again that these are dynamic tools for learning.

 References

Atwell, Nancie. 1987. *In the Middle: Writing, Reading, and Learning with Adolescents*. Portsmouth, NH: Boynton/Cook Publishers Inc.

Collins, Jackie. 1985. *Lucky*. New York, NY: Simon & Schuster.

Fulwiler, Toby. 1987. *The Journal Book*. Portsmouth, NH: Heinemann Educational Books, Inc.

David Seltzer. 1976. *The Omen*. New York, NY: New American Library.

Wouk, Herman. 1983. *Marjorie Morningstar*. New York, NY: Doubleday.

Wyndham, John. 1955, 1975. *The Chrysalids*. London, Eng.: Michael Joseph.

A Community of Teachers

*After fourteen years of teaching grades two and five, **Beverly MacLean** recently spent a year as a resource teacher. In addition to her current teaching, Ms. MacLean is now working with a team of lead teachers in her rural school division to assist with the in-service training for teachers who are taking on a new provincial language-learning curriculum.*

I overheard a teacher in our staffroom exclaiming:

> "I'm so pleased with what's happening in my reading class. My room is busy with small groups of children completing a variety of tasks. One group of children was reading, one group writing in response journals, and several were working on book projects. It works! Readers' Workshop really does work and I love it!"

Her excitement was being voiced by many teachers throughout our school division. While some of us had done a great deal of background reading and had attended professional development sessions dealing with Readers' Workshops, I knew many of us wanted to keep learning all we could about this exciting new strategy. And there were many other teachers who wanted to be introduced to Readers' Workshops. I have always felt a personal need for ongoing informal professional development and remembered being very enthused when an in-service workshop leader had suggested, "If you get a chance, join a Readers' Workshop interest group."

As this thought grew in my mind, I decided to take the first step. I advertised the formation of a teacher interest group in a division-wide newsletter. I hoped the interest group would provide teachers with the opportunity to share their ideas as well as to grow with the Readers' Workshop philosophy. Having anticipated that six to ten teachers would like to become members of the group, I was pleasantly surprised when fifteen eager participants arrived at our first meeting.

Our group is made up of teachers from grades one to six. Some members are veterans of Readers' Workshops and others are just beginning. One teacher commented to the group, "I'm ready. Tell me all you know!" We were on our way as an interest group!

We began our first meeting by sharing experiences. In order to set priorities for further meetings, we each voiced our particular concerns. Newcomers wanted to know everything, from getting started to evaluation. Experienced teachers were eager to act as resource people but also wanted to refine their own skills pertaining to response journals and mini-lessons. Organizational items such as book selections, storage of materials, and space for children to work, all needed to be considered. We questioned what skills in group work and comprehension our students would need in order to be successful with Readers' Workshops. As we reflected on our discussion, we knew we had our agendas for future meetings.

My role as chair of the group is a simple one. At each meeting I try to have something new, such as a just-published teacher's reference or an idea for a mini-lesson, to share with the group. Prior to each gathering, the agenda we have agreed upon is sent out so that members are reminded to prepare questions or bring materials for sharing at the session. The agenda gives us reference points for our meetings, but other topics emerge as we meet. For example, at one meeting one teacher worried, "I seem to be reading the same books to my class year after year. I need some new titles." Thus began informal book talks and discussions of children's literature that have had an impact on us.

As those of us who have experience with Readers' Workshops share our knowledge and experiences with novices to the workshop approach, I find that I am reassessing and reaffirming my own beliefs about Readers' Workshops and about children's learning. I find I have grown tremendously in my repertoire of skills needed for helping children to experience literature. My mini-lessons continue to develop and I have an ever-increasing knowledge of children's books. More important, the enthusiasm we share in the group helps to energize me in the classroom.

Teachers do voice concerns and some have doubts. Quiet reading classrooms have a different look as they become Readers' Workshops. Diverse activities take place at the same time and give the class an appearance of confusion. Class management becomes a concern for some teachers. We share such organizational items as bulletin boards, group diaries, teacher checklists for monitoring the "status-of-the-class," and daily goals in order to help set a structure for these teachers' Readers' Workshop classrooms. We all wonder about how to deal with the child who cannot or will not function in a group. The need to spend time teaching children group interaction skills was one helpful hint.

Teacher expectations for response journals at all grade levels was a priority for our group in our first meetings. We brainstormed what a response journal is and what a response journal is not. We examined what we considered to be good responses at various grade levels and in doing so came to see that children's responses tend to follow a developmental continuum, that is, they tend to mature in complexity and content as the children move through the grades and have more experience with responding.

The definition of what represents "good literature" will be an ongoing topic for our group. In addition, we are determined to give our children the opportunity to experience a variety of appropriate literature forms.

Evaluation of student work is a major concern for many of us. As we listen to one another talk about our workshops and about our children we hear how each person is engaged in observing children learning. We begin to understand what we can be looking for—from the subtle indicators of a child's engagement in a book to the responses of a frustrated group member. I find that my own reactions and my written responses to journal entries are strengthened and expanded by reading other teachers' responses. My ability to evaluate oral reading has been refined just from our discussions about how different students approach difficulties. Nevertheless, as a group we know that our skills of observing children learning will need to be strengthened and refined.

As well as the practical and professional benefits gained by forming an interest group, I have found kindred spirits among the group members. We share, learn, and have fun.

We all chuckled as one grade two teacher told of a little boy's answer when she was taking the status-of-the-class. He said excitedly, "Oh, today we are just disgusting!" She smiled, stifled a laugh, and replied, "Have a good discussion." Many teachers use a tape recorder to help evaluate group discussions. One grade five group showed their creativity in dealing with an absent group member. The boys played their tape before handing it in and apparently decided it was too short. At the end of their discussion, they introduced and left space for their absent member. The tape played on; not a sound could be heard. Finally, in all seriousness, the boys said, "Thank you, Arnold, and that's all for today." Many anecdotes such as these make our discussions very real and bring the enjoyment of teaching close to hand.

Our group is informal, allowing people to come and go according to their interests. Small groups have formed from our large one. Group members who are colleagues meet to discuss yearly school plans and library concerns. Grade one teachers attend some large group sessions, but also find it beneficial to meet with one another to discuss in particular the needs of the beginning reader. We meet at different schools, which has given a variety of people a chance to share their ideas and organization first hand.

Our school division covers a large rural area but the interest group seems to make the distances between us less. It is comforting to know that we are not individuals struggling alone but a group of professionals working together. Because we have an increasing knowledge of how teachers and children handle Readers' Workshops from the primary level to grade six, our interest group adds continuity to reading programs throughout our division. I believe our interest group has really formed a community of teachers. The advice given to me by an in-service workshop leader had been very wise: "If you get a chance, join a Readers' Workshop interest group."

Resources to Bridge Literature and Literacy

Readers' Workshops require that we teachers be knowledgeable about what literature will be interesting and meaningful to our students. We must also be aware of ongoing developments in the understandings of how the process of reading actually works. Like so many other professionals today, we are also constantly challenged to keep up-to-date.

There are, of course, many ways we can become more knowledgeable and stay abreast of new books and research. Our teacher-librarians, for example, can be a major resource in our efforts to keep up-to-date. Books and articles are important resources for providing us with the knowledge we need.

Many of us have found the books and articles listed in this "Resources" section to be of great help in charting our own voyages across the bridge towards literacy. We hope that you, too, will find in the resources listed some works that will help you in your ongoing learning about the process of reading and about the literature that will help you to implement Readers' Workshops in your own classrooms.

The resources listed are divided into two parts: "I. Literature in the Elementary Classroom" and "II. Resources Especially for Secondary Teachers." The resources are annotated and are works that have influenced what those of us using Readers' Workshops are doing and that are relevant to the implementation of Readers' Workshops.

I. Literature in the Elementary Classroom

Compiled by Terry MacKenzie

In this section, we provide an extensive annotated listing of books we have found helpful in implementing our Readers' Workshops. For greater ease of use, the resources are grouped into four subsections. Where appropriate, references are listed in more than one subsection.

The books listed in "1. A Selection of Bibliographies" provide annotations of *children's books and novels* that can be successfully used in classrooms or that can be recommended to parents and guardians for home reading and reading aloud to their children.

The works listed in "2. References About Children's Literature" provide information **about** *the field of children's literature*, helping to expand our own knowledge and understanding about the characteristics and genres of children's literature. Many of the resources listed also contain suggestions for books that can be successfully used in the elementary classroom and provide some teaching strategies.

The emphasis in "3. Teacher Resources on Teaching with Children's Literature" is on the *practical*, helping you to see the ways literature can be used appropriately within language arts programs.

"4. Resources of Particular Interest to Parents" contains some books and pamphlets that will assist parents who want to read with and to their children, and who wish to listen to their children read to them. These works tend to be informative about reading skills and strategies.

1. A Selection of Bibliographies

Ammon, Bette DeBruyne & Gale W. Sherman. 1989. *Handbook for the 1990 Young Reader's Choice Award Nominees*. Pocatello, ID: Beyond Basals.

A guide to the fifteen titles nominated for the 1990 Young Reader's Choice Award of the Pacific Northwest Librarians' Association (PNLA), an award begun in 1940. An in-depth treatment of books for grades four to eight, the *Handbook* includes for each book, the genre(s), theme(s), readability and interest data, author information, plot summary, read-aloud guide, book talks, other books by the author, and a list of books of similar interest. The *Handbook* is published every year.

Boehnlein, Mary M. & Beth H. Hager, Compilers. 1985. *Children, Parents, and Reading: An Annotated Bibliography*. Newark, DE: International Reading Association.

Extensive bibliography on many aspects of the topic. Includes materials for parents and periodicals for children and parents.

Booth, David & Bill Moore. 1988. *Poems Please! Sharing Poetry with Young Children*. Markham, ON: Pembroke Publishers Limited.

Examines the world of children's poetry: why share poetry with children, how poems work, what happens when we read poems, ideas for reading and writing poems. Focuses on the teaching of poetry. Includes an extensive annotated bibliography of poetry — both anthologies of poetry and individual poet's collections.

Booth, David, Larry Swartz & Meguido Zola. 1987. *Choosing Children's Books*. Markham, ON: Pembroke Publishers Limited.

Organized around four categories of books for preschool years (infants to age five), for primary children (ages five to eight), for middle readers (ages eight to eleven), and for young adolescents (ages eleven to fourteen), this highly recommended reference annotates over 1000 titles from North America, the United Kingdom, Australia, and New Zealand. Titles are grouped by a variety of genres and themes, and include read alouds, books for reluctant readers and books for special topic interests. Suitable for teachers and parents.

Children's Choices. Newark, DE: International Reading Association.

Published by the International Reading Association in *The Reading Teacher* each October, this list of 100-plus newly published books is chosen by children as their favourites. Grouped by reading levels: all ages, beginning independent reading, young readers, middle grades, older readers. Annotations and bibliographic details are given for each title. Available from the current IRA catalogue.

Children's Literature Arrangements. Revised 1987. Edmonton Public School Board, Curriculum Department, Language Arts Services.

Consists of thematic bibliographies for kindergarten to grade six, as well as recommended read-aloud and independent reading lists at all seven grade levels.

Davis, James E. & Hazel K. Davis, Ed. 1988. *Your Reading: A Booklist for Junior High and Middle School Students*. Seventh edition. Urbana, IL: National Council of Teachers of English.

Developed for student reference. Two thousand books in sixty-one categories, including fiction, nonfiction, poetry, short stories, drama, and picture books for older readers. Brief descriptions. Includes author and title indexes.

Freeman, Judy. 1984. *Books Kids Will Sit Still For*. Hagerstown, MD: Alleyside Press.

Briefly annotated lists of over 1000 read alouds arranged by grade levels, poetry and folk stories. Includes suggestions for giving book talks, storytelling, dramatics, writing, and cross-curricular teaching.

Gagnon, André & Ann Gagnon. 1988. *Canadian Books for Young People*. Fourth edition. Toronto, ON: University of Toronto Press.

More than 2500 carefully selected and annotated in-print books and magazines for young people up to age eighteen. Arranged by subject. Includes an author-title index. Bilingual. An invaluable tool.

Gillespie, John T. & Corinne J. Naden, Ed. 1990. *Best Books for Children: Pre-School through Grade 6*. Fourth edition. New York, NY: R. R. Bowker.

Excellent, up-to-date reference that evaluates more than 11 000 titles including those published through mid-1989. Entries provide reviews from leading journals for titles after 1985. Includes author, title, illustrator, and subject indexes.

Hearne, Betsy. 1990. *Choosing Books for Children: A Commonsense Guide*. Revised edition. New York, NY: Delacorte Press.

Each chapter covers a particular type, or genre, of book from picture books for reluctant readers to poetry. An annotated bibliography accompanies each chapter. Includes chapters on young adult literature and literacy education. Compact, reliable, superbly written practical handbook for parents and for beginners who may be exploring children's and young adults' literature.

Kimmel, Margaret Mary & Elizabeth Segel. 1983. *For Reading Out Loud! A Guide to Sharing Books with Children*. New York: Delacorte Press. (Also 1984. New York, NY: Dell Publishing Co.)

Filled with activities including how to read aloud and how to introduce books to elementary school students. Contains short summaries of over 140 popular trade books for reading aloud, plus extensive listings of good books by grade and age level. For teachers and parents.

Kohn, Rita T. 1986. *Once Upon—A Time for Young People and Their Books: An Annotated Resource Guide*. Metuchen, NJ: Scarecrow Press Inc.

A guide for professionals to resource materials on print and non-print children's literature. Intended for librarians, media specialists and teachers. Much more extensive than this Resource section!

Landsberg, Michele. 1986. *Michele Landsberg's Guide to Children's Books*. Markham, ON: Penguin Books Canada Limited.

A critical guide to good children's and young adults' books by a writer who cares to help us form our own judgements about books' literary merits. Over 350 topnotch Canadian, American, and British children's books are listed. First part is organized by themes, the second by age groups. Each title is briefly annotated. Deals with questions of sexism, racism, violence, television, encouraging reading, etc. A classic.

Larrick, Nancy. 1982. *A Parent's Guide to Children's Reading*. New York, NY: Bantam Books.

A comprehensive guide on sharing literature with children. Includes annotated lists of books organized under useful headings, such as "History—Fact and Fiction" and "Science and Nature."

McMullan, Kate Hall. 1984. *How To Choose Good Books for Kids*. Don Mills, ON: Addison-Wesley Publishers Limited.

Gives characteristics of books appropriate for children from birth to age eleven. Divided by age groups, each section includes annotations of appropriate fiction books.

Meagher, Joe. 1985. *Readioactive: How To Get Kids Reading for Pleasure*. Markham, ON: Paperjacks. (Now Markham, ON: Distican)

Aimed at parents and teachers of twelve- to sixteen-year-olds who are reluctant or inexperienced readers. Proposes large quantities of paperback reading. Includes 230 titles grouped thematically and rated for difficulty. Annotated.

Moss, Anita & Jon Stott. 1986. *The Family of Stories: An Anthology of Children's Literature*. Toronto, ON: Holt, Rinehart and Winston of Canada Ltd.

Presents stories arranged by traditional genres, which were often oral: folk tales, hero tales and myths; and by more modern literary genres: literary folk tales, literary hero tales, and literary myths. Includes appendices on the picture book and children's novels.

Ryder, Randall J., Bonnie B. Graves & Michael F. Graves. 1989. *Easy Reading: Book Series and Periodicals for Less Able Readers*. Newark, DE: International Reading Association.

A bibliography of forty-four book series and fifteen periodicals. Overview gives a good explanation of factors influencing the difficulty of materials and places the use of such materials into the contexts of the reading process and reading instruction. Some attention to the genres represented by these series.

Stott, Jon. 1984. *Children's Literature from A to Z: A Guide for Parents and Teachers*. New York, NY: McGraw-Hill Inc.

Contains entries on past and present major writers and illustrators for children, as well as entries on major genres such as ABC books, folk tales, poetry, etc. Includes "Tips for Parents and Teachers" at the end of each entry.

Stott, Jon C. & Raymond E. Jones. 1988. *Canadian Books for Children: A Guide to Authors and Illustrators*. Toronto, ON: Harcourt Brace Jovanovitch, Canada.

Includes biographical notes and commentary on 105 authors and illustrators as well as a suggested graded reading list of Canadian books (kindergarten to grade eight). Provides ideas for using books in the classroom. You will find this to be an invaluable resource for using Canadian children's literature.

Sutherland, Zena. 1986. *The Best in Children's Books: The University of Chicago Guide to Children's Literature, 1979–84*. Chicago, IL: University of Chicago Press.

In alphabetical arrangement by author, this useful reference tool provides 1400 reviews of children's books published between 1979 and 1984. Entries include recommended reading level. Six indexes.

Sutherland, Zena & Mary Hill Arbuthnot. 1986. *Children and Books*. Seventh edition. Glenview, IL.: Scott, Foresman & Co.

Includes sections about knowing children and books and exploring types of literature. Offers suggestions for bringing children and books together. Annotated book lists are organized by genre.

Trelease, Jim. 1989. *The New Read-Aloud Handbook*. New York, NY: Penguin USA.

A bestseller, now in its second revised edition, this guide to good books for reading aloud also gives a convincing argument for making reading aloud an established and enjoyable practice in the home. Provides annotations to over 300 books grouped under headings: "Wordless Books," "Predictable Books," "Picture Books," "Short Novels," "Novels," "Poetry Anthologies." Recommends grade ranges.

Wiener, Harvey S. 1988. *Talk with Your Child*. New York, NY: Penguin USA.

This is an excellent book about the importance of conversation in developing the language of children. Includes annotations on fifty books for children that may open the door to that conversation. These annotations are extensive introductions to the author's personal treasury of books.

Wilms, Denise Murcko, Ed. 1987. *A Guide to Non-sexist Children's Books, Volume II: 1976–1985*. Chicago IL: Academy Chicago Publishers.

Authoritative, reliable text offers annotations for more than 600 non-sexist titles arranged alphabetically in three age groups: preschool to grade three, grades four to six and grades seven to twelve. Useful.

Wilson, George & Joyce Moss. 1988. *Books for Children To Read Alone: A Guide for Parents and Librarians*. New York, NY: R. R. Bowker.

Useful tool, organized by grade level, provides "old favourites and newer works" in each section for easy, average, and challenging reading. Wide range of genres. Indexes.

Young Adults' Choices. Newark, DE: International Reading Association.

Published by the International Reading Association in *Journal of Reading* each November, this list of newly published books is chosen by readers from middle, junior and senior high schools as their favourites. Grouped by reading levels: all ages, beginning independent reading, young readers, middle grades, older readers. Annotations and bibliographic details are given for each title. Available from the current IRA catalogue.

2. References About Children's Literature

Applebee, Arthur N. 1978. *The Child's Concept of Story Ages Two to Seventeen*. Chicago, IL: University of Chicago Press.

Examines the potent relationship between stories and the language development of children. Discusses the changing relationships children of different age have with "story."

Arbuthnot, May Hill. 1986. *The Arbuthnot Anthology of Children's Literature*. Glenview, IL: Scott, Foresman & Co.

Looks at the history of children's literature and offers teaching strategies. Includes a massive collection of poetry, folklore, short stories, and some nonfiction, including biography.

Beginning with Excellence: An Adult Guide to Great Children's Reading. (3 cassettes). 1988. Boston, MA: The Horn Book.

Designed for teachers, parents and librarians, the cassettes describe whys and hows of encouraging readers through suggestions of titles and activities. Includes interviews with authors and illustrators, and excerpts from notable books.

Benton, Michael & Geoff Fox. 1985. *Teaching Literature: Nine to Fourteen*. Oxford, Eng.: Oxford University Press.

About teaching poems and stories, including novels. Includes sections on the nature of literary response and literature experiences, and many teaching ideas for authentic work with literature. A must for those of us interested in reader response, especially from grades three to nine!

Bettleheim, Bruno. 1976. *The Uses of Enchantment: The Meaning and Importance of Fairy Tales*. New York, NY: Alfred E. Knopf Inc. Distributed by Random House Inc.

Discusses the significance of fairy tales in meeting and addressing the emotional needs of children.

Cullinan, B. E. 1989. *Literature and the Child*. Second edition. New York, NY: Harcourt Brace Jovanovich Inc.

Outstanding books are reviewed with ideas for introducing them to readers. Seven major genres are considered.

Donelson, Kenneth & Alleen Nilson. 1989. *Literature for Today's Young Adult*. Third edition. Glenview, IL: Scott, Foresman & Co.

A junior high reference but useful to elementary teachers as a resource for characteristics of genres, including sections on Utopian literature and science fiction which other references sometimes overlook. Also includes sections on plot, theme, character, point of view, tone, and style.

Egoff, Sheila, G.T. Stubbs & L. F. Ashley, Ed. 1980. *Only Connect: Readings on Children's Literature*. Second edition. Toronto, ON: Oxford University Press.

Critical essays featuring historical, social and generic approaches. Includes articles by writers such as C.S. Lewis and Tolkien, and by scholars such as Roger Lancelyn Green and John Rowe Townsend.

Glazer, Joan I. 1986. *Literature for Young Children*. Second edition. Columbus, OH: Charles E. Merrill. (Now Merrill Publishing Co.)

Focuses on the opportunities books offer for supporting young children's language, intellectual, personality, social and moral, and aesthetic and creative development. Introduces a range of literature. Designed for teachers of preschool and primary children. Specific teaching strategies offered.

Georgiou, Constantine. 1969. *Children and Their Literature*. Englewood Cliffs, NJ: Prentice-Hall.

Another fine source on children's literature, especially its divisions or genres such as fantasy, realism, folk and fairy tales, myths, fables and legends, and history and information in children's literature. Annotated bibliographies, although a bit dated.

Huck, Charlotte S., Susan Hepler, & Janet Hickman. 1987. *Children's Literature in the Elementary School*. Fourth edition. New York, NY: Holt, Rinehart and Winston Inc.

Discusses types of children's literature and teaching methods. Includes extensive bibliographies. One of the most comprehensive reference books on children's literature. Note in particular the chapter on "Understanding Children's Response to Literature." Amply illustrated.

Kimmel, Margaret Mary & Elizabeth Segel. 1983. *For Reading Out Loud! A Guide to Sharing Books with Children*. New York, NY: Delacorte Press. (Also 1984. New York, NY: Dell Publishing Co.)

Filled with activities including how to read aloud and how to introduce books to elementary school students. Contains short summaries of over 140 popular trade books for reading aloud, plus extensive listings of good books by grade and age level. For teachers and parents.

Meek, Margaret, Aidan Warlow & Griselda Barton, Ed. 1977. *The Cool Web: The Pattern of Children's Reading*. London, Eng.: The Bodley Head.

Essays that explore in various ways the role of the child reader in literary experience and the nature of narrative.

Monson, Dianne L., Ed. 1985. *Adventuring with Books*. Urbana, IL: National Council of Teachers of English.

Recommends 1700 children's books published between 1981 and 1984. Headings include curricular areas (science, social studies, fine arts, sports) and genres (poetry, biography, fantasy). Reviews look at literary and artistic quality as well as at books' appeal to children.

Moss, Anita & Jon Stott. 1986. *The Family of Stories: An Anthology of Children's Literature*. Toronto, ON: Holt, Rinehart and Winston of Canada Limited.

Presents stories arranged by traditional genres which were often oral: folk tales, hero tales and myths; and by more modern literary genres: literary folk tales, literary hero tales, and literary myths. Includes appendices on the picture book and children's novels. Explanatory introductions and appendices provide additional information about children's literature. Extensive bibliographies of criticism books are provided. Fine resource.

Norton, Donna. 1987. *Through the Eyes of a Child: An Introduction to Children's Literature*. Columbus, OH: Charles E. Merrill. (Now Columbus, OH: Merrill Publishing Co.)

This comprehensive text includes a history of children's literature, criteria for evaluating and selecting children's literature, and chapters on each of the genres, as well as chapters on multi-ethnic literature and artists and illustrations. Teaching suggestions, activities, and annotated bibliographies are included in each chapter.

Rosenblatt, Louise. 1938, 1983. *Literature as Exploration*. Fourth edition. New York, NY: The Modern Language Association of America.

A major source on the view of reading as a transactional process between reader and text. An academic reference rather than a "how-to."

Rosenblatt, Louise. 1978. *The Reader, the Text, the Poem: The Transactional Theory of the Literary Work*. Carbondale, IL: Southern Illinois University Press.

Louise Rosenblatt paved the way for work done in response theory. An accessible book that clearly explains transactional theory and its implications for the classroom.

Stewig, John Warren. 1980. *Children and Literature*. Boston, MA: Houghton Mifflin Co.

Deals with illustration; alphabet, picture and wordless picture books; genres such as traditional literature, poetry, historical fiction, biography, contemporary fiction, fantasy; special interests: animal stories, mystery, sports and science fiction; information books; planning a literature curriculum.

Stott, Jon. 1984. *Children's Literature from A to Z: A Guide for Parents and Teachers*. New York, NY: McGraw-Hill Inc.

Contains entries on past and present major writers and illustrators for children, as well as entries on major genres such as ABC books, folk tales, poetry, etc. Includes "Tips for Parents and Teachers" at the end of each entry.

Sutherland, Zena & Mary Hill Arbuthnot. 1986. *Children and Books*. Seventh edition. Glenview, IL.: Scott, Foresman & Co.

Includes sections about knowing children and books and exploring types of literature. Also includes suggestions on bringing children and books together. Annotated book lists are organized by genre.

3. Teacher Resources on Teaching with Children's Literature

Applebee, Arthur N. 1978. *The Child's Concept of Story Ages Two to Seventeen*. Chicago, IL: University of Chicago Press.

Examines the potent relationship between stories and the language development of children. Discusses the changing relationships children of different age have with "story."

Arbuthnot, May Hill. 1986. *The Arbuthnot Anthology of Children's Literature*. Glenview, IL: Scott, Foresman & Co.

Looks at the history of children's literature and offers teaching strategies. Includes a massive collection of poetry, folklore, short stories, and some nonfiction, including biography.

Atwell, Nancie, Ed. 1990. *Workshop 2 by and for teachers: Beyond the Basals*. Portsmouth, NH: Heinemann Educational Books, Inc.

A second collection of pieces by teachers based upon their classroom practices. These articles have a strong focus on the use of literature in classrooms, on students' responses to literature and on how the teachers' own knowledge informed their practices. Many of the articles give insights into the teacher-writers' own adaptations of Readers' Workshops.

Atwell, Nancie, Ed. 1989. *Workshop 1 by and for teachers: Writing and Literature*. Portsmouth, NH: Heinemann Educational Books, Inc.

Articles by teachers and for teachers. Very powerful presentation of stories of success.

Atwell, Nancie. 1987. *In the Middle: Writing, Reading, and Learning with Adolescents*. Portsmouth, NH: Boynton/Cook Publishers Inc.

Talks about writing and reading process classrooms at junior high level, but the theory and practice described are applicable to elementary grades. Includes many examples from classroom experiences. Note in particular the author's section on "Reading Workshop."

Balaam, Jan & Brian Merrick. N.d. *Exploring Poetry: 5–8*. Sheffield, Eng.: National Association for the Teaching of English.

Suggests various ways to introduce poems to young children and provides activities for bringing children close to those poems. Includes poems, activities and extensions. Illustrated. Practical.

Benton, Michael & Geoff Fox. 1985. *Teaching Literature: Nine to Fourteen*. Oxford, Eng.: Oxford University Press.

About teaching poems and stories, including novels. Includes sections on the nature of literary response and experiences in reading literature, and provides many teaching ideas for authentic work with literature. A must for those of us interested in reader response, especially from grades three to nine!

Booth, David & Bill Moore. 1988. *Poems Please! Sharing Poetry with Young Children*. Markham, ON: Pembroke Publishers Limited.

Examines the world of children's poetry: why share poetry with children, how poems work, what happens when we read poems, ideas for reading and writing poems. Focuses on the teaching of poetry. Includes an extensive annotated bibliography of poetry—both anthologies and individual poet's collections.

Butler, Andrea & Jan Turbill. 1984. *Towards a Reading-Writing Classroom*. Portsmouth, NH: Heinemann Educational Books, Inc.

Excellent handbook of ninety pages by Australian educators and language consultants. Describes teachers' classrooms that closely link reading and writing theory and practice. Includes workable ideas for routines, classroom organization, creating big books, shared-book experiences, and the like.

Calkins, Lucy McCormick. 1986. *The Art of Teaching Writing*. Portsmouth, NH: Heinemann Educational Books, Inc.

A must read for any teacher who anticipates or is using a workshop approach! See her section on reading-writing connections, especially the chapters on reading process and the writing-reading workshop.

Calkins, Lucy McCormick with Shelley Harwayne. 1991. *Living Between the Lines*. Toronto, ON: Irwin Publishing.

There are many reasons why teachers of all ages may want to read this book, but, with Readers' Workshops in mind, starting places might be the section on text-sets on page 132 or Chapter 11 dealing with picture books in the reading-writing workshops of older children. You'll be hooked!

Chambers, Aidan. 1986. *Introducing Books to Children*. Portsmouth, NH: Heinemann Educational Books, Inc.

Includes excellent approaches and ideas on presenting literature to children. Of particular interest for those using a Readers' Workshop format in the classroom.

Collie, Joanne & Stephen Slater. 1987. *Literature in the Language Classroom*. Cambridge, Eng.: Cambridge University Press.

An excellent resource book of ideas and activities written for secondary teachers yet adaptable for use by elementary teachers. Includes formats for lessons that integrate reading, discussion, and writing.

Corcoran, Bill & Emrys Evans, Ed. 1987. *Readers, Texts, Teachers*. Upper Montclair, NJ: Boynton/Cook Publishers Inc.

A collection of eleven essays explaining reader response theory, arguing its relevance to young, developing readers, and indicating appropriate classroom practices. Be sure to read Bill Corcoran's "Teachers Creating Readers."

Cullinan, Bernice E. 1989. *Literature and the Child*. Second edition. New York, NY: Harcourt Brace Jovanovich Inc.

Outstanding books are reviewed with ideas for introducing them to readers. Seven major genres are considered.

Cullinan, Bernice E., Ed. 1987. *Children's Literature in the Reading Program*. Newark, DE.: International Reading Association.

A milestone publication from the International Reading Association and a bestseller! A must-have for elementary/middle school teachers.

Provides many approaches for beginning a literature-based program and/or for enriching and extending the use of literature. Sections deal with a rationale for using children's literature, reading programs using such literature in kindergarten to grade three, grades four to six, and grades six to eight. Interspersed with specific teaching suggestions and recommended books.

Freeman, Judy. 1984. *Books Kids Will Sit Still For*. Hagerstown, MD: Alleyside Press.

Briefly annotated lists of over 1000 read alouds arranged by grade levels, poetry and folk stories. Includes suggestions for book talking, storytelling, dramatics, writing, and cross-curricular teaching.

Fulwiler, Toby, Ed. 1987. *The Journal Book*. Portsmouth, NH: Heinemann Educational Books, Inc.

Gives a wealth of information regarding the use of journals across subject/content areas. Don't ignore the math and science chapters.

Glazer, Joan I. 1986. *Literature for Young Children*. Second edition. Columbus, OH: Charles E Merrill. (Now Columbus, OH: Merrill Publishing Co.)

Focuses on the opportunities books offer for supporting young children's language, intellectual, personality, social and moral, and aesthetic and creative development. Introduces a range of literature. Designed for teachers of preschool and primary children. Specific teaching strategies offered.

Hackman, Susan. 1987. *Responding in Writing: The use of exploratory writing in the literature classroom*. Sheffield, Eng.: National Association for the Teaching of English.

Serves as a practical and example-filled guide to the introduction of exploratory writing in the classroom. Includes a chapter on reading journals and one on writing literature essays.

Hancock, Joelie & Susan Hill. 1987. *Literature-based reading programs at work*. Richmond Hill, ON: Scholastic-TAB Publications.

Australian teachers tell their stories about beginning literature-based programs in years two through seven. Several specific programs are described, ranging from theme to genre to author programs. Practical ideas abound, especially about organizing, selecting materials and implementing programs built around real books. Very friendly book with workable, practical ideas.

Hansen, Jane. 1987. *When Writers Read*. Portsmouth, NH: Heinemann Educational Books, Inc.

Describes classrooms in which reading instruction is accomplished using a process approach. Connections between reading and writing are made. Useful for teachers using a Readers' Workshop model.

Harste, Jerome, Kathy G. Short & Carolyn Burke. 1988. *Creating Classrooms for Authors*. Portsmouth, NH: Heinemann Educational Books, Inc.

Presents the concept of an authoring curriculum in which students build their engagement with literacy activities from life experiences, uninterrupted reading and writing, and the guidance of the teacher. Provides many useful teaching strategies such as "Say Something" and "Literature Circles."

Hart-Hewins, Linda & Jan Wells. 1988. *Borrow A Book: Your Classroom Library Goes Home*. Richmond Hill, ON: Scholastic Canada Ltd.

For teachers who wish to consider ways to get books into the home and to encourage parent-child reading at home. Describes a project that began in a kindergarten-grade one class in Toronto.

Hill, Susan. 1986. *Books Alive! Using Literature in the Classroom*. Melbourne, Australia: Nelson.

Presents ideas for literature-based reading programs organized around response, author, story or great books. Contains many suggestions for teachers. Includes author biographies, activities, bibliographies. Accessible.

Hopkins, Lee Bennett. 1987. *Pass the Poetry, Please!, The Revised Edition*. New York, NY: Harper & Row, Publishers Inc.

Another fine source about the sharing and teaching of poetry with students. Includes useful biographical notes on twenty contemporary poets, ideas for working with poems, and many references to poetry anthologies.

Johnson, Terry D. & Daphne R. Louis. 1987. *Literacy Through Literature*. Richmond Hill, ON: Scholastic Canada Ltd.

Many classroom suggestions for using real books in the elementary classroom. Includes rationale and suggestions for a literature-based curriculum, and provides valuable teaching suggestions. Makes reference to many children's books in the teaching examples.

Kobrin, Beverly. 1988. *Eyeopeners!: How To Choose and Use Children's*

Books About Real People, Places, & Things. New York, NY: Penguin USA.

Practical guide on the use of nonfiction books for kindergarten through grade eight. Discusses how to judge a book and suggests steps for motivating children to read. Useful annotated list of over 500 books with tips on how to use.

Language Arts. Urbana, IL: National Council of Teachers of English.

Monthly journal on the teaching of the Language Arts. Includes reviews of children's books and profiles on writers. The April issue is devoted to literature in the Language Arts.

McConaghy, June. 1990. *Children Learning Through Literature: A Teacher Researcher Study*. Portsmouth, NH: Heinemann Educational Books, Inc.

An easy-to-read book based upon the author's grade one teaching experiences with a literature-based program. Chapters deal with various topics, including a day in the classroom, children learning through stories, working on home-school relationships, and the teacher as learner.

Meek, Margaret. 1991. *On Being Literate*. London, Eng.: The Bodley Head.

A companion volume to *Learning To Read*, this book places learning to read and write into the larger context of schooling. In particular, it can help parents and teachers who wonder how to talk about what "counts as reading" in their homes or schools.

Meek, Margaret. 1982. *Learning To Read*. London, Eng.: The Bodley Head.

Discusses the major stages in learning to read. Very readable itself.

Meek, Margaret, Aidan Warlow & Griselda Barton, Ed. 1977. *The Cool Web: The Pattern of Children's Reading*. London, Eng.: The Bodley Head.

Essays that explore in various ways the role of the child reader in literary experience and the nature of narrative.

Moffett, James. 1968. *Teaching the Universe of Discourse*. Boston, MA: Houghton Mifflin Co.

Examines a sequence of narrative types developed from the viewpoint that authors take particular stances towards their readers. Based on the notion of narrative being central for children until formal thinking and abstract categorizing develop.

Moss, Anita & Jon Stott. 1986. *The Family of Stories: An Anthology of Children's Literature*. Toronto, ON: Holt, Rinehart and Winston of Canada Ltd.

The appendices, in particular, deal with teaching interpretive skills to children, and include additional bibliographies of interest to teachers: books on teaching as well as journals and periodicals. Presents stories arranged by traditional genres which were often oral: folk tales, hero tales and myths; and by more modern literary genres: literary folk tales, literary hero tales, and literary myths. Includes appendices on the picture book and children's novels.

Norton, Donna. 1987. *Through the Eyes of a Child: An Introduction to Children's Literature*. Columbus, OH: Charles E. Merrill. (Now Columbus, OH: Merrill Publishing Co.)

This comprehensive text includes a history of children's literature, criteria for evaluating and selecting children's literature, and chapters on each of the genres, as well as chapters on multi-ethnic literature and artists and illustrations. Teaching suggestions, activities, and annotated bibliographies are included in each chapter.

Parsons, Les. 1990. *Response Journals*. Markham, ON: Pembroke Publishers Limited.

A valuable handbook on the use of response journals. It places response journals in the context of personal response to literature, to read alouds, to media and in the context of small group discussions.

Peetoom, Adrian. 1986. *Shared Reading: Safe Risks with Whole Books*. Richmond Hill, ON: Scholastic Canada Ltd.

One of the first of Scholastic's short teacher references (32 pages), this reference provides useful strategies for teachers of less able readers in grades two to six in the presentation and use of chapter books in the classroom.

Peterson, Ralph & Maryann Eeds. 1990. *Grand Conversations: Literature Groups in Action*. Richmond Hill, ON: Scholastic-TAB Publications Ltd.

A fine resource for teachers who wish to consider a range of ways to include literature in their reading programs. Focuses on the role of the home, group sharing of stories, extensive reading and intensive reading. Also provides brief introductions to literary elements as a help to teachers working with literature in the elementary grades.

Power, Brenda Miller & Ruth Hubbard, Ed. 1991. *Literacy in Process: The Heinemann Reader*. Portsmouth, NH: Heinemann Educational Books, Inc.

Over thirty articles have been collected in this anthology which represents a diversity of views in current thinking about literacy theory and practice. Theorists and practitioners represented include Louise Rosenblatt, Donald Graves, Lucy Calkins, Patrick Shannon, Leslie Funkhauser, and Toby Fulwiler. This is an excellent collection of excerpts, essays, interviews and research reports for elementary teachers who are thinking about the links between practice and theory.

Purves, Alan C. & Dianne L. Monson. 1984. *Experiencing Children's Literature*. Glenview, IL: Scott, Foresman and Co.

Helps teachers understand what reading literature is all about and why it is important in schools. Based on the transactional theory of Louise Rosenblatt, the book traces roots of children's literature in folklore and myth, examines major genres of fiction and poetry, examines the nature of reading, and assists with teachers' curricular decisions on book selection and literature programs. Includes many useful references to writers and sources.

Reading Teacher, The. Newark, DE: International Reading Association.

Appearing ten times a year, this journal for elementary teachers focuses on the teaching of reading with periodic articles on the use of literature in that teaching. Includes reviews of children's books and professional books. Also includes the yearly listing of Children's Choices.

Routman, Regie. 1991. *Invitations: Changing as Teachers and Learners*. Toronto, ON: Irwin Publishing.

Designed to support and encourage teachers who are consciously and conscientiously working to become whole language teachers, Routman's book invites them to try a wide range of literacy activities with their students. Routman is aware of degrees of teacher control so suggests transitions towards more student control. Chapters on responding to literature provide a wealth of structured suggestions that could lead into successful Readers' Workshops. Excellent professional references.

Routman, Regie. 1988. *Transitions from Literature to Literacy*. Portsmouth, NH: Heinemann Educational Books, Inc.

An excellent resource for teachers moving into teaching reading and writing from a literature base in grades one through three. Based on a teacher's personal experiences, the text includes many very specific examples and practical suggestions. Includes annotated lists of resources for teachers: professional books and articles, literature activity resources, and book lists for grades one, two, and three. Provides suggestions for parent involvement and parent information sheets.

Shapiro, Jon, Ed. 1979. *Using Literature and Poetry Affectively*. Newark, DE: International Reading Association.

A series of articles grouped around the issues of attitude towards reading, uses of literature and uses of poetry.

Sloan, Glenna Davis. 1984. *The Child as Critic: Teaching Literature in Elementary and Middle Schools*. Second edition. New York, NY: Teachers College Press.

Summarizes the literary theories of Northrop Frye concerning the structural principles of literature and shows how teachers may implement these theories in teaching literature in elementary classes.

Stewig, John Warren. 1980. *Read To Write: Using Children's Literature as a Springboard for Teaching Writing*. Second edition. New York, NY: Holt, Rinehart and Winston Inc.

The entire premise of this book is using children's literature as a springboard for the teaching of writing. Deals with oral language, characterization, setting, plot, figurative language, poetry, and editing. While this is a most comprehensive resource on developing children's skills in writing fiction and poetry through a literature-based program, it precedes the concepts of a writing workshop. May be very valuable for mini-lessons.

Stewig, John Warren & Sam Leaton Sebesta, Ed. 1989. *Using Literature in the Elementary Classroom*. Urbana, IL: National Council of Teachers of English.

Seven articles chosen to assist the application of the children's literature in the classroom movement. Includes chapters on learning to read with picture books, literature in the composing process, and literature across the curriculum. Note Helen Fesenthal's "The Tradebook as an Instructional Tool: Strategies in Approaching Literature." Although the approach in this text is quite teacher-centred, the articles may assist with designing mini-lessons for teachers using Readers' Workshops. All articles contain many references to specific children's books.

Stott, Jon. 1984. *Children's Literature from A to Z: A Guide for Parents and Teachers*. New York, NY: McGraw-Hill Inc.

Contains entries on past and present major writers for children, as well as entries on types of genres such as ABC books, folk tales, poetry, etc. Includes "Tips for Parents and Teachers" at the end of each entry.

Thomas, Ron & Andrew Perry. 1984. *Into Books: 101 Literature Activities for the Classroom*. Melbourne, Australia: Oxford University Press.

Recommends informal activity and discussion around books that teachers read to children. Suggests a framework for literature themes at three levels: ages five to seven, eight to nine, and ten to twelve. Includes studies of novels, picture story books, poetry, and works of specific authors.

Waterland, Liz. 1985. *Read with Me: An Apprenticeship Approach to Reading*. Stroud, Glos.: The Thimble Press.

At forty-eight pages, a wonderful little exposition on teaching children to read naturally. Waterland works from Ken Goodman's and Frank Smith's views of reading process, arguing that readers need real books from the beginning and a teacher who understands learning to read as an apprenticeship to the craft of reading.

4. Resources of Particular Interest to Parents

Barton, Bob. 1986. *Tell Me Another: Storytelling and Reading Aloud at Home, at School and in the Community*. Markham, ON: Pembroke Publishers Limited.

Consisting of stories, rhymes and songs, the text offers excellent ideas on how to find, choose and present them and how to incorporate music and drama into storytelling and oral reading. Extensive annotated bibliography.

Beginning with Excellence: An Adult Guide to Great Children's Reading. (3 cassettes). 1988. Boston, MA: The Horn Book.

Designed for teachers, parents and librarians, the cassettes describe whys and hows of encouraging readers through suggestions of titles and activities. Includes interviews with authors and illustrators, and excerpts from notable books.

Boegehold, Betty D. 1984. *Getting Ready To Read.* New York, NY: Ballantine Books.

At 258 pages, this is quite an extensive explanation of the whys and ways for parents to help their children get ready for reading, but it provides many valuable activities and resources. The text is divided into age groups from birth to six-year-olds. Many children's books are referenced.

Booth, David, Larry Swartz & Meguido Zola. 1987. *Choosing Children's Books.* Markham, ON: Pembroke Publishers Limited.

Organized around four categories of books for preschool years (newborns to age five), for primary children (ages five to eight), for middle readers (ages eight to eleven), and for young adolescents (ages eleven to fourteen), this highly recommended reference annotates over 1000 titles from North America, the United Kingdom, Australia, and New Zealand. Titles are grouped by a variety of genres and themes, and include read alouds, books for reluctant readers and books for special topic interests. Suitable for teachers and parents.

Butler, Dorothy. 1988. *Babies Need Books. Second edition.* London, Eng.: Penguin.

Presents a guide for parents in selecting books for children from the earliest months to age six. Focuses on the emotional and cognitive significance of the interactions between parents, babies and books. Includes many specific suggestions for books, with annotations.

Butler, Dorothy. 1986. *Five to Eight.* London, Eng.: The Bodley Head.

Picks up where the first edition of *Babies Need Books* left off and describes children's reading preferences at these ages. Advocates a relaxed approach to the subject of learning to read, and attempts to persuade parents to continue reading aloud to their children. The extensive bibliography is largely, but not exclusively, British.

Butler, Dorothy. 1975. *Cushla and Her Books.* Auckland, NZ: Hodder and Stoughton.

This book, which speaks to parents of children with special needs, describes the story of love and devotion of Cushla's parents and the role books played in her development.

Butler, Dorothy & Marie Clay. 1982. *Reading Begins at Home: Preparing Children for Reading Before They Go to School.* Portsmouth, NH: Heinemann Educational Books, Inc.

In forty-three pages, overviews possible home reading activities for preschoolers and beginning readers. Shows parents how they can prepare their preschoolers for learning in groups at school by providing one-to-one learning in everyday situations.

Carlsen, G. Robert. 1980. *Books and the Teenage Reader*. Second edition. New York, NY: Harper & Row, Publishers Inc.

Comprehensive guide to literature for teenagers, including a discussion of all reading material from the classics to the adolescent novel. Includes bibliographies with brief descriptions of each book.

Cohen, Miriam. 1977. *When Will I Read?* New York, NY: Dell Yearling. (Now New York, NY: Dell Publishing Co.)

A book for grade one readers with a humourous message for parents!

Cutting, Brian. 1985. *Talk Your Way to Reading: Helping Your Child with Reading*. Toronto, ON: Ginn Publishing Canada Inc.

In sixty-four pages, liberally sprinkled with coloured photos, the author speaks directly to parents about ways to work with their young children on talking, listening, writing and reading. The games and activities allow for learning in a natural and easy way. Highly recommended.

Doake, David B. 1988. *Reading Begins at Birth*. Richmond Hill, ON: Scholastic-TAB Publications.

Presents parents with actual examples of children and books becoming the best of friends. Demonstrates the kind of environment that encourages reading development.

Freeman, Judy. 1984. *Books Kids Will Sit Still For*. Hagerstown, MD: Alleyside Press.

Briefly annotated lists of over 1000 read alouds arranged by grade levels, poetry and folk stories. Includes suggestions for book talking, storytelling, dramatics, writing, and cross-curricular teaching.

Gross, Jacquelyn. 1986. *Make Your Child a Lifelong Reader: A Parent-Guided Program for Children of All Ages Who Can't, Won't, or Haven't Yet Started To Read*. Los Angeles, CA: Jeremy P. Tarcher Inc. Distributed by St. Martin's Press, New York.

An excellent resource for parents and teachers who help parents, primarily because the author supports real reading activities, not the reading of words or sounds without meaning. Provides goals and suggestions that are grouped by age (infancy to six, six to eleven, twelve to eighteen). Includes reading lists for each age group. Highly recommended.

Hearne, Betsy. 1990. *Choosing Books for Children: A Commonsense Guide*. Revised edition. New York, NY: Delacorte Press.

Each chapter covers a particular type, or genre, of book from picture books for reluctant readers to poetry. An annotated bibliography accompanies each chapter. Includes chapters on young adult literature and literacy education. Compact, reliable, superbly written practical handbook for parents and for beginners who may be exploring children's literature.

Hill, Mary W. 1989. *Home: where reading and writing begin*. Richmond Hill, ON: Scholastic Canada Ltd.

A readable little book about the partnerships between parents and young children in learning to read and write. Includes ideas about listening to children read and insights about children learning from their own writing.

Kimmel, Margaret Mary & Elizabeth Segel. 1983. *For Reading Out Loud! A Guide to Sharing Books with Children*. New York, NY: Delacorte Press. (Also 1984. New York, N.Y.: Dell Publishing Co.)

Filled with activities including how to read aloud and how to introduce books to elementary school students. Contains short summaries of over 140 popular trade books for reading aloud, plus extensive listings of good books by grade and age level. For teachers and parents.

Kobrin, Beverly. 1988. *Eyeopeners!: How To Choose and Use Children's Books About Real People, Places, & Things*. New York, NY: Penguin USA.

Practical guide on the use of nonfiction books for kindergarten to grade eight. Discusses how to judge a book and suggests steps for motivating children to read. Useful annotated list of over 500 books with tips on how to use.

Landsberg, Michele. 1986. *Michele Landsberg's Guide to Children's Books*. Markham, ON: Penguin Books Canada Limited.

A critical guide to good children's and young adults' books by a writer who cares to help us form our own judgements about books' literary merits. Over 350 topnotch Canadian, American, and British children's books are listed. First part is organized by themes, the second by age groups. Each title is briefly annotated. Deals with questions of sexism, racism, violence, television, encouraging reading, etc. A classic.

Larrick, Nancy. 1982. *A Parent's Guide to Children's Reading*. New York, NY: Bantam Books.

A bestselling comprehensive guide on sharing literature with children. Includes annotated lists of books organized under useful headings, such as "History — Fact and Fiction" and "Science and Nature." Offers descriptions of children's reading preferences by age.

Lipson, Eden Ross. 1988. *New York Times Parent's Guide to the Best Books for Children*. New York, NY: Times Books.

Comprehensive, illustrated, and annotated compilation of nearly 1000 titles from wordless picture books to young adult. Includes thirty indices by topic and category.

McMullan, Kate Hall. 1984. *How To Choose Good Books for Kids*. Don Mills, ON: Addison-Wesley Publishers Limited.

Gives characteristics of books for children from birth to age eleven. Divided by age groups, each section includes annotations of appropriate fiction books. Brief, at eighty pages, yet practical.

Meagher, Joe. 1985. *Readioactive: How To Get Kids Reading for Pleasure*. Markham, ON: Paperjacks. (Now Markham, ON: Distican.)

Aimed at parents and teachers of twelve- to sixteen-year-olds who are reluctant or inexperienced readers, the text proposes large quantities of paperback reading. Includes 230 titles grouped thematically and rated for difficulty. Annotated.

Meek, Margaret, 1991. *On Being Literate*. London, Eng.: The Bodley Head.

A companion volume to the earlier *Learning to Read*, this text places learning to read and write into the larger context of schooling. In particular, it can help parents and teachers who wonder how to talk about what "counts as reading" in their homes or schools. Written for parents.

Meek, Margaret. 1982. *Learning To Read*. London, Eng.: The Bodley Head.

Discusses the major stages in learning to read. Very readable itself.

Parent Booklets. Newark, DE: International Reading Association.

A series of sixteen to twenty-four page booklets focused on answering questions parents often ask. Filled with sound, practical advice. Titles as of late summer 1991 included:

Beginning Literacy and Your Child by Steven and Linda Silvern
Helping Your Child Become a Reader by Nancy L. Roser

How Can I Prepare My Young Child for Reading? by Paula C. Grinnell
You Can Help Your Young Child with Writing by Marcia Baghban
Creating Readers and Writers by Susan Mandel Glazer
Encouraging Your Junior High Student To Read by John Shefelbine
Ayude a su nino con la escritura is a Spanish translation of
Baghban's *You Can Help Your Young Child with Writing*

Parent Brochures. Newark, DE: International Reading Association.

Also available from IRA are a series of small brochures focusing on
practical reading concerns of parents and on ways for parents to help
their children. These Parent Brochures are also available in French.
Some titles are

Good Books Make Reading Fun for Your Child
Summer Reading Is Important
You Can Encourage Your Child To Read
You Can Help Your Child Connect Reading to Writing
You Can Help Your Child in Reading by Using the Newspaper
You Can Use Television To Stimulate Your Child's Reading Habits

Pellowski, Anne. 1987. *The Family Storytelling Handbook: How To Use
Stories, Anecdotes, Rhymes, Handkerchiefs, Paper and Other Objects to
Enrich Family Traditions*. New York, NY: Macmillan Publishing Co.

Concise, well-organized presentation of why, when, and what
kinds of tales to tell. Includes seventeen carefully selected, tested
and workable multicultural tales involving simple props. Highly
recommended.

Reed, Arthea J. S. 1988. *Comics to Classics: A Parent's Guide to Books for
Teens and Preteens*. Newark, DE: International Reading Association.

This good, practical resource discusses how to encourage young
people to read, how to make television a literary experience, etc.
Focuses on pleasure rather than a required reading approach.
Annotated bibliography includes an excellent, diverse selection of
titles.

Stoll, Donald R., Ed. 1989. *Magazines for Children*. Newark, DE:
Educational Press Association of America and International Reading
Association.

A guidebook to more than 125 children's periodicals, aimed at
infants on up to teenagers. A handy bibliography for parents and
teachers.

Stott, Jon. 1984. *Children's Literature from A to Z: A Guide for Parents
and Teachers*. New York, NY: McGraw-Hill Inc.

Contains entries on past and present major writers for children, as well as entries on types of genres such as ABC books, folk tales, poetry, etc. Includes "Tips for Parents and Teachers" at the end of each entry.

Taylor, Denny & Dorothy S. Strickland. 1986. *Family Storybook Reading*. Richmond Hill, ON: Scholastic-TAB Publications.

Practical suggestions on how to incorporate storybook reading into family life, and why to do so. Includes suggestions for ways parents can help children learn about reading and writing from storybook reading. Natural and sensible methods. Photos. Recommended.

Trelease, Jim. 1989. *The New Read-Aloud Handbook*. New York, NY: Penguin USA. Co-distributed by International Reading Association.

A bestseller, now in its second revised edition, this guide to good books for reading aloud also gives a convincing argument for making reading aloud an established and enjoyable practice in the home. Provides annotations to over 300 books grouped under headings: Wordless Books, Predictable Books, Picture Books, Short Novels, Novels, Poetry Anthologies. Recommends grade ranges. Includes a chapter on the effects of television.

Villiers, Una. 1989. *LUK MUME LUK DAD I KAN RIT*. Richmond Hill, ON: Scholastic-TAB Publications.

Chronicles the early steps taken by a group of inner-city schoolchildren as they learn to write — naturally. Richly illustrated guide to early writing stages.

Wiener, Harvey S. 1988. *Talk with Your Child*. New York, NY: Penguin USA.

This is an excellent book about the importance of conversation in developing the language of children. It also includes annotations on fifty books for children that may open the door to that conversation. These annotations are extensive introductions to the author's personal treasury of books.

Wilms, Denise Murcko, Ed. 1987. *A Guide to Non-sexist Children's Books, Volume II: 1976–1985*. Chicago, IL: Academy Chicago Publishers.

This authoritative, reliable text offers annotations for more than 600 non-sexist titles arranged alphabetically in three age groups: preschool to grade three, grades four to six and grades seven to twelve. Useful.

Wilson, George & Joyce Moss. 1988. *Books for Children To Read Alone: A Guide for Parents and Librarians*. New York, NY: R. R. Bowker.

Useful tool, organized by grade level; provides old favourites and newer works in each section for easy, average, and challenging reading. Includes wide range of genres, and indices.

II. Resources Especially for Secondary Teachers

Compiled by Kathleen Weir

We have found the following books to be good introductions for secondary teachers who are exploring the implications of reader response or Readers' Workshops in their classrooms. The writing that results from responding to reading in secondary literature programs is an integral part of a response program. Many of the books listed in this section serve to place student writing-as-response within the theoretical framework of reader response.

Anson, Chris M., Ed. 1989. *Writing and Response: Theory, Practice, and Research*. Urbana, IL: National Council of Teachers of English.

Note especially "Transactional Theory and Response to Student Writing" by Robert E. Probst on pages 68–79, and "The Writer's Memo: Collaboration, Response, and Development" by Jeffrey Sommers on pages 174–186.

Applebee, Arthur N. 1978. *The Child's Concept of Story Ages Two to Seventeen*. Chicago, IL: University of Chicago Press.

Examines the potent relationship between stories and the language development of children. Discusses the changing relationships children of different age have with "story."

Atwell, Nancie, Ed. 1990. *Workshop 2 by and for teachers: Beyond the Basals*. Portsmouth, NH: Heinemann Educational Books, Inc.

A second collection of pieces by teachers based upon their classroom practices. These articles have a strong focus on the use of literature in classrooms, on students' responses to literature and on how the teachers' own knowledge informed their practices. Many of the articles give insights into the teacher-writers' own adaptations of Readers' Workshops.

Atwell, Nancie, Ed. 1989. *Workshop 1 by and for teachers: Writing and Literature*. Portsmouth, NH: Heinemann Educational Books, Inc.

Articles by teachers and for teachers. Very powerful presentation of stories of success.

Atwell, Nancie. l987. *In the Middle: Writing, Reading, and Learning with Adolescents*. Portsmouth, NH: Boynton/Cook Publishers Inc.

A must read for teachers at any level. The opening chapter "Learning How to Teach" addresses the fundamental issue of control in the classroom. Note also her section on Reading Workshop. Includes many examples from classroom experiences.

Benton, Michael & Geoff Fox. 1985. *Teaching Literature: Nine to Fourteen*. Oxford, Eng.: Oxford University Press.

About teaching poems and stories, including novels. Includes sections on the nature of literary response and experiences in reading literature, and provides many teaching ideas for authentic work with literature. A must for teachers interested in reader response.

Berthoff, Ann E. 1981. *The Making of Meaning: Metaphors, Models, and Maxims for Writing Teachers*. Upper Montclair, NJ: Boynton/Cook Publishers Inc.

Ann Berthoff shoots straight from the hip with this no-nonsense blend of theory and practice. Berthoff stresses the importance of a theoretical framework to support practice in the classroom. She explores the composing/thinking process as a creative imaginative act and relates it to art and music.

Booth, David, Larry Swartz & Meguido Zola. 1987. *Choosing Children's Books*. Markham, ON: Pembroke Publishers Limited.

Organized around four categories of books for preschool years (newborns to age five), for primary children (ages five to eight), for middle readers (ages eight to eleven), and for young adolescents (eleven to fourteen), this reference annotates over 1000 titles from North America, the United Kingdom, Australia, and New Zealand. Titles are grouped by a variety of genres and themes, and include books for reluctant readers and books for special topic interests. Suitable for teachers and parents.

Calkins, Lucy McCormick. 1986. *The Art of Teaching Writing*. Portsmouth, NH: Heinemann Educational Books, Inc.

A must read for any teacher who anticipates or is using a workshop approach! See her section on reading-writing connections, especially the chapters on reading process and the writing-reading workshop.

Calkins, Lucy McCormick with Shelley Harwayne. 1991. *Living Between the Lines*. Toronto, ON: Irwin Publishing.

There are many reasons why teachers of all ages may want to read this book, but, with Readers' Workshops in mind, a starting place might be the section on text-sets on page 132. You'll be hooked!

Carlsen, G. Robert. 1990. *Books and the Teenage Reader*. Second edition. New York, NY: Harper & Row, Publishers Inc.

Comprehensive guide to literature for teenagers, including a discussion of all reading material from the classics to the adolescent novel. Includes bibliographies with brief descriptions of each book.

Children's Choices. Newark, DE: International Reading Association.

Published by the International Reading Association in *The Reading Teacher* each October, this list of 100-plus newly published books is chosen by children as their favourites. Grouped by reading levels: all ages, beginning independent reading, young readers, middle grades, older readers. Annotations and bibliographic details are given for each title. Available from the current IRA catalogue.

Collie, Joanne & Stephen Slater. 1987. *Literature in the Language Classroom*. Cambridge, Eng.: Cambridge University Press.

An excellent resource book of ideas and activities written for secondary teachers. Includes formats for lessons that integrate reading, discussion, and writing.

Corcoron, Bill & Emerys Evans. 1987. *Readers, Texts, Teachers*. Upper Montclair, NJ: Boynton/Cook Publishers Inc.

A collection of essays explaining reader response theory, arguing its relevance to young, developing readers, and indicating appropriate classroom practices. Be sure to read Bill Corcoron's "Teachers Creating Readers."

Donelson, Kenneth & Alleen Nilson. 1989. *Literature for Today's Young Adult*. Third edition. Glenview, IL: Scott, Foresman & Co.

Useful as a resource for characteristics of genres, including sections on Utopian literature and science fiction which other resources sometimes overlook. Also includes sections on plot, theme, character, point of view, tone, and style.

English Journal. Urbana, IL: National Council of Teachers of English.

Monthly journal written by and for English teachers of all levels. The Journal publishes descriptions of classroom practice that are supported by anecdotal detail, theory, or professional literature.

Farrell, Edmund J. & James R. Squire, Ed. 1990. *Transactions with Literature: A Fifty-Year Perspective*. Urbana, IL: National Council of Teachers of English.

Dedicated to Louise Rosenblatt (see listings below), this collection of essays reaffirms the impact of Rosenblatt's work on classroom teachers.

Fulwiler, Toby, Ed. 1987. *The Journal Book*. Portsmouth, NH: Heinemann Educational Books, Inc.

Gives a wealth of information regarding the use of journals across subject/content areas. Don't ignore the math and science chapters.

Fulwiler, Toby. 1987. *Teaching with Writing*. Portsmouth, NH: Boynton/Cook Publishers Inc.

Discusses the use of writing to learn across content areas.

Gagnon, Andre & Ann Gagnon. 1988. *Canadian Books for Young People*. Fourth edition. Toronto, ON: University of Toronto Press.

More than 2500 in-print books and magazines for young people up to age eighteen are carefully selected and annotated and arranged by subject. Includes an author-title index. Bilingual. An invaluable tool.

Gross, Jacquelyn. 1986. *Make Your Child a Lifelong Reader: A Parent-Guided Program for Children of All Ages Who Can't, Won't, or Haven't Yet Started to Read*. Los Angeles, CA: Jeremy P. Tarcher Inc. Distributed by St. Martin's Press Inc., New York, NY.

An excellent resource for parents and teachers who help parents, primarily because the author supports real reading activities, not the reading of words or sounds without meaning. Provides goals and suggestions grouped by age (infancy to age six, ages six to eleven, and ages twelve to eighteen). Includes reading lists for each age group. Highly recommended.

Hearne, Betsy. 1990. *Choosing Books for Children: A Commonsense Guide*. Revised edition. New York, NY: Delacorte Press.

Each chapter covers a particular type, or genre, of book from picture books for reluctant readers to poetry. An annotated bibliography accompanies each chapter. Includes chapters on young adult literature and literacy. Compact, reliable, superbly written practical handbook for parents and beginners at exploring children's literature.

Landsberg, Michele. 1986. *Michele Landsberg's Guide to Children's Books*. Markham, ON: Penguin Books Canada Limited.

A critical guide to good children's and young adults' books by a writer who cares to help us form our own judgements about books' literary merits. Over 350 topnotch Canadian, American, and British children's and young adult books are listed. First part is organized by themes, the second by age groups. Each title is briefly annotated. Deals with questions of sexism, racism, violence, television, encouraging reading, etc. A classic.

Meagher, Joe. 1985. *Readioactive: How To Get Kids Reading for Pleasure*. Markham, ON: Paperjacks. (Now Markham, ON: Distican.)

Aimed at parents and teachers of twelve- to sixteen-year-olds who are reluctant or inexperienced readers. Proposes large quantities of paperback reading. Includes 230 titles grouped thematically and rated for difficulty. Annotated.

Moffett, James. 1983. *Teaching the Universe of Discourse*. Boston, MA: Houghton Mifflin Co.

Examines a sequence of narrative types developed from the viewpoint that authors take particular stances towards their readers. Based on the notion of narrative being central for children until formal thinking and abstract categorizing develop.

Murray, Donald M. 1987. *Write To Learn*. New York, NY: Holt, Rinehart and Winston Inc.

Donald Murray's easy-going style is very accessible as he continues to explore writing in all its facets.

Murray, Donald M. 1985. *A Writer Teaches Writing*. Second edition. Boston, MA: Houghton Mifflin Co.

A sensitive look at response to writing. A must for teachers trying to pull together the theoretical implications of a response-centred reading program with the writing done in their classrooms.

Newkirk, Thomas, Ed. 1990. *To Compose: Teaching Writing in High School and College*. Second edition. Portsmouth, NH: Heinemann Educational Books, Inc.

A solid look at teaching writing, this book deals not only with the triumphs but with the difficulties facing teachers. The editor's question and answer segments tie together articles by authors such as Cormier and Stafford with familiar names such as Atwell, Murray, Perl, Probst, Fulwiler, and Flower.

Newman, Judith A., Ed. 1985. *Whole Language*. Portsmouth, NH: Heinemann Educational Books, Inc.

Deals with philosophical stance, beliefs about whole language and implications for practice.

Parent Booklets. Newark, DE: International Reading Association.

A series of sixteen- to twenty-four-page booklets focused on answering questions parents often ask. Filled with sound, practical advice. Current titles include:

You Can Encourage Your High School Student To Read by Jamie Myers
Creating Readers and Writers by Susan Mandel Glazer
Encouraging Your Junior High Student To Read by John Shefelbine

Parsons, Les. 1990. *Response Journals*. Markham, ON: Pembroke Publishers Limited.

A valuable handbook on the use of response journals. It places response journals in the context of personal response to literature, to read alouds, to media and in the context of small group discussions.

Power, Brenda Miller & Ruth Hubbard, Ed. 1991. *Literacy in Process: The Heinemann Reader*. Portsmouth, NH: Heinemann Educational Books, Inc.

Over thirty articles have been collected in this anthology that represents a diversity of views in current thinking about literacy theory and practice. Theorists and practitioners represented include Louise Rosenblatt, Donald Graves, Lucy Calkins, Patrick Shannon, Leslie Funkhauser, and Toby Fulwiler. This is an excellent collection of excerpts, essays, interviews and research reports for teachers who are thinking about the links between practice and theory.

Probst, Robert. 1988. *Response and Analysis: Teaching Literature in Junior and Senior High School*. Portsmouth, NH: Boynton/Cook Publishers Inc.

Probst makes Rosenblatt's transactional theory (see listings below) accessible by providing practical suggestions for implementing transactional theory.

Reed, Arthea J. S. 1988. *Comics to Classics: A Parent's Guide to Books for Teens and Preteens*. Newark, DE: International Reading Association.

This good, practical resource discusses how to encourage young adults to read, how to make television a literary experience, etc. Focuses on pleasure reading rather than a required reading approach. Annotated bibliography includes an excellent, diverse selection of titles.

Romano, Tom. 1987. *Clearing the Way—Working with Teenage Writers*. Portsmouth, NH: Heinemann Educational Books, Inc.

Romano shares his experience of working with writers in the classroom.

Rosenblatt, Louise. 1938, 1983. *Literature as Exploration*. Fourth edition. New York, NY: The Modern Language Association of America.

A major source on the view of reading as transaction. In the Foreword to the fourth edition, Alan Purves stresses Rosenblatt's vision of a classroom in which teacher and student share honestly. An academic reference rather than a "how to."

Rosenblatt, Louise. 1978. *The Reader, the Text, the Poem: The Transactional Theory of the Literary Work*. Carbondale, IL: Southern Illinois University Press.

Louise Rosenblatt paved the way for work done in response theory. An accessible book that clearly explains transactional theory and its implications for the classroom.

Stoll, Donald R., Ed. 1989. *Magazines for Children*. Newark, DE: Educational Press Association of America and International Reading Association.

A guidebook to more than 125 children's periodicals, aimed at infants on up to teenagers. A handy bibliography for parents and teachers.

Wilms, Denise Murcko, Ed. 1987. *A Guide to Non-sexist Children's Books, Volume II: 1976–1985*. Chicago, IL: Academy Chicago Publishers.

This authoritative, reliable text offers annotations for more than 600 non-sexist titles arranged alphabetically in three age groups: preschool to grade three, grades four to six, and grades seven to twelve. Useful.

Young Adults' Choices. Newark, DE: International Reading Association.

Published by the International Reading Association in *Journal of Reading* each November, this list of newly published books is chosen by readers from middle, junior, and senior high schools as their favourites. Grouped by reading levels: all ages, beginning independent reading, young readers, middle grades, older readers. Annotations and bibliographic details are given for each title. Available from the current IRA catalogue.